Acclaim

Autism Tomorrow is a book that I guarantee will grab you in the first few minutes, and then inform, educate, and move you to a level of understanding of autism that I did not think possible. I am much more emotionally attuned and adequately informed on autism after reading this fine work of Karen Simmons, Bill Davis and the other experts who contributed to this book.

—*Pennsylvania State Senator, Mike Brubaker, Member of the Autism Caucus and Children's Health Caucus*

In this compelling and articulate volume, the authors tell you how to educate and support autistic children, and give you a window into how to love them too. It should be the go-to book for parents addressing the confusion attendant on an autism spectrum diagnosis.

—*Andrew Solomon, National Book Award Winner and Pulitzer Prize Finalist, author of The Noonday Demon: An Atlas of Depression, and the forthcoming A Dozen Kinds of Love: Discovering The Horizontal Family*

In the world of tomorrow, people with autism will be encouraged to live successful and productive lives using their strengths. Sufficient resources will be devoted to removing barriers that prevent them from leading lives of authentic success and fulfillment. This book is a must!

—*Dr. Stephen Shore, Professor and Author of Beyond the Wall: Personal Experiences With Autism and Asperger's Syndrome; Understanding Autism For Dummies; Ask and Tell: Self-Advocacy and Disclosure for People on the Autism Spectrum*

This is the finest, most advanced book on autism and real life available. Once you pick it up, you'll keep reading, as it both enlightens and inspires, while giving the solid tips you need to help your child truly flourish in today's and tomorrow's world. Get a copy for your child's teacher, your doctor, your parents, and most importantly, yourself.

—*Frank Barnhill, M.D., Family Practitioner*
Author, Mistaken For ADHD
www.drhuggiebear.com

D0110211

Autism Tomorrow is one book I'll recommend to all my patients who have, or know of a child or adult with autism. The tips in this book are cutting-edge, and far beyond measure. You'll learn how to maintain your parental sanity, how to get help for college, and everything in between.

—*Stephen Guffanti, M.D. Family Practitioner*
Author, Does Your Child Really Have ADHD?
Creator, Rocket Phonics, www.RocketPhonics.com and www.DrDyslexic.com

Every family who wants to encourage, nourish, and be a champion for their child with autism needs this book. *Autism Tomorrow* will be your most trusted resource for a long time to come.

—*Rebecca Kochenderfer*
Author, Homeschooling and Loving It
Editor, www.Homeschool.com

Autism Tomorrow reminds us that we are not alone in this journey. The practical advice shared by Karen, Bill and the other contributors is invaluable and a must read for anyone trying to grasp what daily life is like with Autism, and how to appropriately address it.

—*Joel Manzer*
Parent of a child with autism, www.Autisable.com

As the population of individuals with autism rapidly increases, so rises the urgency to cultivate a cultural competency that affords each person opportunities to participate and contribute authentically. *Autism Tomorrow* is a timely and thorough resource to support this noble endeavor.

—*William Stillman, self-advocate and award-winning author of Autism and the God Connection and Empowered Autism Parenting*
www.williamstillman.com

Autism Tomorrow

The Complete Guide To Help Your Child Thrive In The Real World

Karen L. Simmons
Bill Davis

Exceptional Resources, Inc. provides their book titles at quantity discounts to schools and other organizations. Please e-mail karen@exceptionalresources.com for more information. To obtain additional copies of *Autism Tomorrow*, visit www.AutismTomorrow.com.

Exceptional Resources, Inc.

1425 Broadway #444

Seattle, WA 98122

www.AutismToday.com

Cover Design

Susan Simmons, www.SimmonsGallery.com
Dunn+Associates, www.dunn-design.com and

Interior Design of Book

Susan Simmons, www.SimmonsGallery.com

Editor
Pat Wyman, www.HowToLearn.com

ISBN: 978-0-9724682-2-0
Distributed to the trade by Exceptional Resources, Inc.

Printed in the United States of America

1 3 5 7 9 10 8 6 4 2

Dedication

I dedicate this book to our sons and daughters, who will share its gems with their sons and daughters and perfect it over time. *Autism Tomorrow* belongs to our cherished children and their future; may they be empowered by our acceptance and deep love of who they are today, and who they will be tomorrow...

Karen L. Simmons

I share this dedication because these people have shared their lives with me, and have made me a better person. For Kathleen Ann Cannon-Davis, my wife, I dedicate this book to you, not for the miracles you perform, but for who you are. To my children, Danielle, Jessica, Christopher, and Rocco, and grandchildren, Rinoa and Roxas, you are always the light of my life. And, with a deep love and commitment, I dedicate *Autism Tomorrow*, not only to the autism community, but to all readers.

Bill Davis

Acknowledgements

From Karen L. Simmons: My sincere, heartfelt appreciation goes out to my wonderful, loving family. Thank you to my husband, Jim Sicoli, our children, Kimberly, Matthew, Christina, Jonathan, Stephen, and Alex, who have so graciously shared me with my intense addiction to autism solutions, and who have been the inspiration for all that I am and do! To my extended family, my sweet sister, Susan Simmons, my loving mother, Mitzi Briehn, my dear mother-in-law, Josephine Sicoli, my generous sister-in-law Anna, and her family, Julia and Christopher Ehli.

Also, a huge thank you to my staff, Shane Lamotte, Larry Draut, and others, who provided their professional knowledge, expertise, and understanding to enhance this book in unique and wonderful ways. Honestly, I don't know how I'd get through the day without you.

To The Center for AAC & Autism; We all thank you for your sponsorship in printing this book. It is with your tremendous belief, trust, and faith in our children with autism and in our organization that will help reach so many people around the world delivering the message of hope and possibilities towards the future. Your generosity will have ripple effects always...

To Bill Davis, my co-author; you are the inspiration who makes this book a pivotal, one-of-a-kind statement in the world of autism today! You live with autism 24/7, and your son, Chris, radiates so much love, he's a teacher for us all. Bill, you and your wife Kate continue to give of yourselves to the autism community in many amazing ways. Thank you for sharing this journey with me and my family!

To all the fabulous contributors in this book, their warm words of wisdom, their passion and their desire to see the world change towards the better for all those with autism and the lives they touch.

To Pat Wyman, thank you so much for everything you have done to help bring this book to realization, including with corporate sponsorship and advocating for the readers at every turn as the book's editor. Your efforts will help thousands of families, teachers, caregivers, and others who need it most. You are a real champion for children, as well as a remarkable expert in learning and reading. Your contributions to both our books help all children, and it is such a delight to work with you. You always hold such a big vision, are deeply kind, generous and ever optimistic. Thank you!

To my sweet sister, Susan; your talents are beyond measure. You are truly a renaissance woman of vision! You not only did the graphics, layout, formatting, and a huge portion of the cover for this book, you designed the magical 'pearls of wisdom', which jump off the page and inspire us all. You do everything with such love and care and I'm always in awe. As an artist, your heart and soul shows in your graphics, design, and creative writing. I want people to know the real you, and how talented you are. To my dear readers, you can see more of Susan's work at www.SimmonsGallery.com

And to Connie Anderson, of Words and Deeds (www.wordsanddeedsinc. com); you without a doubt had a real gift of reviewing and condensing the manuscript, from the reader's point of view. Your work is invaluable and greatly appreciated. And to our proofreaders, Lea Hill, Jamie Harmon, Thelma Kattan, Mitzi Briehn, Jean Erwin, and Beverly Ballina; thank you all so much for volunteering your time and expertise.

From Bill Davis: I want to acknowledge my wife's Uncle Kevingerarrd for having such a tremendous influence on her life, and thank the Tirone family for "adopting us", Mateo for being such a great reader, Ita for laughing at my jokes, Elizabethtown Middle School, Andrew Solomon, Gotham, Eric and Jennie, Loran, and Sharon, M&T Bank, Everyone at Bube's Brewery, Liz Carotto , Joey and Lisa, Matt and the other Matt, Mrs. Rapp, Mrs. Kimmel and all my friends in the world of disabilities. Thank you to Karen Simmons, my friend, partner, and mentor. For Susan Simmons, you've created such a beautiful book cover, and made this book a true work of art on the inside, especially with your unique 'pearls'. Thank you.

A special note to Pat Wyman; I want to thank you so much, both as the Editor, and contributing author, who joined this project at an extremely critical time. You breathed life into this book, and will bring educators, authors, caregivers, and parents together, because you created something unique and special that will shine throughout the autism community. You nurtured, sacrificed, dedicated your time, expertise, and heart to this book. I am very proud to be involved, and am forever thankful to you Pat, for the love you gave *Autism Tomorrow*.

About the Authors

Autism Tomorrow is co-authored by Karen L. Simmons and Bill Davis, both parents of a child with autism. Simmons and Davis have become national experts, spokespersons, and advocates for those with autism. Each contributing author shares their expertise and deep commitment for you and your child's happiness and success, today and in the future.

Karen Simmons

A gemologist by trade, Simmons switched gears to help her real gems, her six children. Once her son, Jonnathan was diagnosed with autism, she devoted her life to helping him and others with autism become their personal best. Simmons' first book, *Little Rainman: Autism Through the Eyes of a Child,* was written from three-year-old Jonny's perspective to help his teachers, siblings, and other parents understand his uniqueness. Highly articulate, Jonny speaks for so many who cannot, as the thousands who have read *Little Rainman* have told us.

Karen's love and passion to help those with autism led her to create more resources, write books, found the website, www.AutismToday.com, host conferences and ultimately become one of the world's leading clearinghouses on information and help for those with autism and Asperger's syndrome. As CEO of Autism Today, she hosts expert classes designed for parents, educators, doctors, therapists, and those who serve the autism and special needs community.

As co-author of *Chicken Soup for the Soul, Children with Special Needs* with Jack Canfield, Mark Victor Hansen, and Heather McNamara, Karen also empowers others to share their heartwarming stories. Her son, Alex, was diagnosed with ADHD, making two of her six children the inspiration for all her work.

Karen authored several other titles: *Artism: Art by Those with Autism, The Autism Experience: Stories of Hope and Love, Peace of Mind for Autism CD; Autism From The Soul CD, Surrounded By Miracles,* plus the Amazon bestseller and Book Of The Year In The Medicine Category, *The Official Autism 101 Manual.* Her books have received critical acclaim from media sources such as Fox News, Global News, PBS, ABC's View from the Bay, and Woman's World Magazine.

Bill Davis

Bill Davis began speaking for and representing his son, Chris, to give him a voice. He quickly became a stellar advocate for children and adults with autism. Bill is the author of two books: *Breaking Autism's Barriers: A Father's Story* and *Dangerous Encounters: Avoiding Perilous Situations with Autism*.

Davis speaks throughout the country at universities and before Congress. He has trained hundreds of Emergency Service Responders, served as an expert witness, and written numerous articles for autism journals. Bill is the former president of the Harrisburg (Pennsylvania) Chapter of The Autism Society of America (ASA), a representative for Unlocking Autism, resident safety expert for Autism Today and the recipient of Temple University's 'End the Victim's Silence' Advocacy Award.

Bill's late wife Jae had a tremendous affect on what he knows. When she died in 2001, Chris was just eight years old and their daughter Jessica was thirteen.

Jae was responsible for many innovative, therapeutic programs. She designed one of the first in-home classrooms in the country. She was stoic and unyielding with awards and scholarships in her honor. Jae was honored by The Pennsylvania State Senate and the city of Lancaster. The service agency, I.U. 13, initiated The Jae Davis Parent Memorial Award, which sends 10 families a year to The Penn State Summer Autism Conference. The Jae Davis Intern Program at Franklyn and Marshall College and the Organization for Autism Research (O.A.R.) present the Jae Davis Award for Community Service every year in Washington D.C. Congressman Jim Greenwood spoke of her accomplishments before a session of Congress on the first anniversary of her death.

Foreword

Dear Reader,

I am a man with autism, who uses the information so lovingly presented in this book, to lead a full, happy, and productive life. When you read these words, know that you're holding a precious gift, which will guide you and your child into an extraordinary future.

The autism community is very fortunate to have such informed, creative, empathetic, and action-oriented people like Karen Simmons, Bill Davis and the others who contributed to this book. You will want to read every word – more than once – because each unique idea and tip will enhance you and your child's life, now and forever.

Autism affects everyone's future and nearly everyone knows, or knows of, a person with autism. As the prevalence of autism grows, enlightening, and inspiring books like *Autism Tomorrow* expand our knowledge to make the existence for the autism community so much easier.

Readers, today you have a guiding light – *Autism Tomorrow*. Let this book be your lighthouse to use, share, and get involved to make the world a better place for people with autism. One person can make a difference, as so many people have proven to us. Advocate and empower those with autism, now and tomorrow, using the material, concepts, and information in this book.

Thank you Karen, Bill, The Center For AAC & Autism, and all the rest of the experts for creating this forward-looking and very much-needed book. And, thank you, dear reader, for bringing these meaningful words to life as they jump off the page when you take them to heart. You are living with autism and your life will be better, as you follow the advice and live the love residing inside this book.

Read some, rest, act, and read some more… I am right here with you.

Warmly,
Dr. Stephen Shore, man with autism
Professor of Special Education at Adelphi University
International Consultant, Presenter on issues related to the Autism Spectrum

Contents

Introduction

What Are The Biggest Questions This Book Answers About Making The Transition To Adulthood?

- How can I provide a financially sound future for my child?
- What kind of work can my child do?
- How do I help make any job situation successful for both my child and the employer?
- How can I help my child's employer and employees understand what autism is and how to use its gifts?
- Should my child go to college and/or get some kind of technical training?
- What do I need to know about independent living situations?
- What community resources are available for my child and family?
- What about my child's care when I can no longer take care of her?
- What kind of long-term help will he need, and what is available?
- How do I help my child, of any age, deal with bullying?
- What should I know about fitness, reading, writing, and communication?
- How can nutritional choices and supplementation help my child reach his full potential?

Autism Tomorrow addresses these questions and many more. Finally, you have a comprehensive resource that provides support for your child's smooth transition to adulthood.

What Is Autism?

According to the Autism Society of America's website, autism is a complex developmental disability that typically appears during the first three years of life and affects a person's ability to communicate and interact with others. Autism is a certain set of behaviors, referred to as a "spectrum disorder", that affects individuals differently and to varying degrees. There is no known single cause for autism, but increased awareness and funding can help families fund the interventions they need.

Autism is a treatable condition. Children do not "outgrow" autism, but studies show that early diagnosis and intervention lead to significantly improved outcomes. (From www.autism-society.org)

In Autism Today's previous book, *The Official Autism 101 Manual*, which won the IPPY Book Of The Year in the Medicine Category award, we wrote that people on the autism spectrum generally have great difficulty making friends and understanding social rules.

They typically have just one or only a few interests, activities or physical movements, in which they engage repeatedly. They may or may not have mental retardation and/or a marked delay in language, although even those who use superficial language may have problems being socially fluent.

As your child grows into adulthood, we know that you'll have lots of questions about how to make that transition as easy and smooth as possible. The experts and people in this book with autism will help you successfully explore the answers to all of your questions.

What is Asperger's Syndrome?

According to the Diagnostic and Statistical Manual of Mental Disorders, fourth edition text revised, or DSM-IV-TR, Asperger's disorder is a developmental disorder. It is at the higher-functioning end of the autism spectrum, and people such as Dr. Stephen Shore and Dr. Temple Grandin, authors in this book, have Asperger's Syndrome.

"Asperger's disorder, which is also called Asperger's Syndrome (AS) or autistic psychopathy, belongs to a group of childhood disorders known as pervasive developmental disorders (PDDs) or autistic spectrum disorders. The essential features of Asperger's disorder are severe social interaction impairment and restricted, repetitive behavior and activities."

Autism Tomorrow serves you best by bridging the gap in autism's future, so you have access to the most helpful and up-to-date information, as well as to the trusted experts who live and understand and care about your life.

Chapter 1

In the Beginning

Chapter 1
In the Beginning

The Facts: As of April 2010, the Centers for Disease Control (CDC) website reports that an average of one in 110 children are diagnosed with autism, resulting in hundreds of thousands of people who need information and services immediately.

...but it takes a child with special needs to raise the consciousness of a village

—Elaine Hall

The Need: Autism rates exponentially increased since the mid-eighties, and thousands of families have a child with autism who are reaching adulthood without a comprehensive resource to help them make that transition.

Autism Tomorrow gives you the comprehensive resource and life guide you need to help your child make a smooth transition into adulthood.

When you have questions about whether your child can work, go to college, live independently, date, get married, have children, be safe, have a secure financial future, or any one of a hundred others, the experts in this book will help you with important decisions on how to proceed. The goal is to help your child not only survive, but thrive in the real world.

We've combined well-researched information and weave in two families' real-life stories about how they handle all the challenges for their sons. One story is about Karen's son, Jonathan, diagnosed with high-functioning autism and refers to himself as Asperger's, and the other is about Bill's son, Chris, who is on the other end of the spectrum, with a more severe form of autism.

You'll read this book, crying one minute and laughing the next, yet always full of hope for your child and his future.

As you continue, you'll discover this is a book of real love and understanding, along with a roadmap for your child's future, no matter where he or she is on the spectrum. This comprehensive manual is for parents, educators, professionals, caretakers, first responders, people around you, and all people with autism. It has practical lists of things to do and not to do, beginning with when your child is young, and later, going out into the world. The topics include education, special training, independent living, college, jobs, families and many more.

We know that everyday life can be challenging when you have a child with autism, and some of the most difficult decisions relate to making plans for your child's care, whether you are around or not. You'll want to know who will care for your child, where she will live and how his or her lifestyle is funded. You'll also want to know more about what your child's daily life will be like and what kinds of documentation you'll need to implement today to ensure your child's best interests.

Families with autism in common can share joys, fears, challenges, and hopes, all within the covers of the book you're holding.

As Bill so eloquently talks about his son, Chris, throughout this book, telling stories, some about great pain, others about joy, he says it best:

> *Suddenly, I am swept up in the beauty of the moment. My son glances up and smiles at me. That is his gift, his special skill. He taught me about life. I am blessed. Chris brought simplicity into my life. He gave me a new vision.*

Relentless Persistence: Making Autism Work
Karen L. Simmons

My sister-in-law insisted I take my son, Jonathan, for an evaluation. When I heard the word autism, I was in a total state of denial. Not my son! But, rather than stick my head in the sand, I decided to prove others wrong by going ahead, not listening to their nonsense, and enrolling him in early intervention. After all, it couldn't hurt him.

Surely, they would recognize that Jonny (Jonathan) was a perfect, so-called, normal child. Eventually, however, the truth about Jonny's disability became obvious, and my decision for early intervention turned out to be the best possible thing for him.

I learned that kids with autism have a different perception of feelings. When Jonny was little, he didn't like to be hugged or touched, and even arched his back when I tried to pick him up. He didn't demand nearly the amount of attention as the other kids. When he went on the bus to school, he didn't hug me or wave good-bye. I took it personally when he pushed me away. I didn't think he had feelings for many years, because he didn't show them.

However, Jonny did have feelings. I realized that when I taught him how to ride a bike. One day, he zipped down the street and across a busy road. If a car had been coming, it would have hit him. I got angry and ran to him screaming, "Jonathan, do you know what you just did? You could have been killed!"

He asked, "What?" Then I said, "You drove your bike across that busy road without even looking to see if a car was coming." He said, "Sorry, Mom." I said, "Sorry doesn't cut it!" Great big tears began to roll down his cheeks. "You hurt my feelings", he said!

That was a first. He was upset because I said, "Sorry doesn't cut it."

Jonathan Sicoli turns 20 in 2010. He is attending the local computer college and says he is, at long last, learning something in school. He loves what he's learning, loves his siblings, his life, and is still the "life of the party." There is never a dull moment with Jonny, as we cannot possibly predict what he is going to do or say next.

People love and like Jonny, and he tells us he is incredibly happy. He knows he has autism, has appeared on television talking about it, and is fine with it. He says, "I wouldn't have it any other way, frankly!" And nor would we.

The important thing, when you have a child with autism, is relentless persistence. This makes autism work for you, and not against you. Persist with questions, and remain forever hopeful. Research new treatment options, attend conferences, on and offline, and connect with other families who have kids with autism too.

In *Autism Tomorrow*, we dig deep to help you answer your questions and include tremendously important subjects, such as:

1. The family dynamic
2. Siblings
3. Hygiene
4. Fitness
5. Safety
6. Women's issues and exams
7. Puberty
8. Bullying
9. Sexual abuse
10. Financial planning
11. School and reading solutions
12. IEPs, IPPs
13. Career training
14. First responders
15. Retailers
16. Special trusts
17. Advocacy
18. School bus drivers
19. Dating
20. Growing older and the future, And much more...

Ultimately, we want you to celebrate the future with us. We give you a roadmap of possibilities, and want you to make informed decisions regarding the direction and intention you have for your child's life. You are holding the guide, tailor-made, to do just that.

In addition, we interviewed top experts, asking what the future of autism means to them. These "Pearls of Wisdom," comments are from Elaine Hall, Dr. Stephen Shore, Dr. Temple Grandin, Jan Randall, Dr. Carolyn T. Bruey, William Stillman, Dr. Tony Attwood, Dr. Kathleen Quill, Donna Williams, Dr. Robert Naseef, Gail Stein, ACSW, Nancy H. Cale, Dr. Barry M. Prizant, Keri Bowers, Tiffany Sandlin, Shannon Johnson, Jennifer Parsons, Leighanne Spitzer, Eric Chessen, Pat Wyman, M.A., and Andrew Solomon.

How Can You "Fix It" If You Don't Know What is Wrong?

The thing about autism is you don't know what's wrong until you finally accept your child as is, and enter their world. This is when things move, and you notice changes that not only make your day, but your life. Here's a funny story that shows what I mean.

Acknowledged by his fellow speaking professionals as "America's Number One Humorous Speaker," Dr. Charles W. Jarvis, DDS, tells this story about a man going to a pet store to buy a bird.

A man goes into the pet store to buy a pet bird. He sees dozens of caged birds with tiny price tags dangling from their little legs. He scans each price tag one by one: $5, $5, $5, $50! "Hmmm," he wonders. "This $50 bird looks like all of the others. What could be so special about this one?" He asks the store clerk. The clerk replies that this one is very special because it can talk. The shopper is impressed enough that he buys this special talking bird and takes it home.

The very next day he returns, disappointed. "The bird didn't talk." The clerk asks, "Did he look in his little mirror?" "Little mirror? I didn't buy a mirror. Does he need a mirror?"

"Of course," replies the clerk. "He looks in his little mirror and sees another bird in there. He thinks he's not alone and starts to sing, starts to talk. You've got to have a mirror." This sounds reasonable, so the customer buys a mirror and leaves.

The next day he is back again, disgruntled. "The bird looked in his little mirror, but he still didn't talk." "Well," ponders the clerk, "did he run up and down his little ladder?" "Does he need a ladder?"

"Of course," replies the clerk. "Don't you feel better after you exercise? When your little bird runs up and down his little ladder, those endorphins start pumping in his little brain. Makes him want to sing. Makes him want to talk. Got to have a ladder."

"How much is a ladder?" "It's $12.95." "Give me a ladder." And off goes the customer. The next day he is back with a scowl on his face. "The bird walked up and down his little ladder. He looked in his little mirror. But he still didn't talk."

The clerk listens to the angry customer and then asks, "Did he swing on his little swing? You see, when the bird swings, it makes him think he's back in nature. Makes him want to sing. Makes him want to talk."

"How much is a swing?" The customer grudgingly buys the swing and leaves. But the very next day he is back again, angrier than ever. "The bird swung on his little swing. He ran up and down his little ladder. He looked in his little mirror. But he still didn't sing and he still didn't talk."

Hmm, thinks the clerk. "Did he tinkle his little bell?" The customer doesn't even wait for an explanation. Determined to see this out to its conclusion, he grabs a little bell, throws some money on the counter and storms off. You guessed it. The very next day he is back again. "The bird's dead!" he exclaims. "Dead?" "Yup, dead! His little feet stick up in the air. He got up this morning healthy as could be. He looked in his little mirror. He tinkled his little bell. He ran up and down his little ladder. He swung on his little swing. And then, just before he keeled over and died, he looked over at me, a little tear forming in his little eye, and he finally spoke to me. The little bird asked, 'Didn't they sell birdseed?'"

Okay, so our children don't need bells, ladders or mirrors, but they do need many things "typical children" don't need to manage their daily lives.

The point of this story is that without really knowing what our child needs, we can throw money, programs, training, ideas, concepts, doctors and more programs at them, to say nothing about the time it takes to do all these things. We can't "fix it" if we don't know what is wrong. We can't decide who is best to treat autism if we don't know who the experts are to help us. We can't figure out how to work with schools and other professionals, determine our family's needs, or weave our way through the always looming financial demands of this thing called autism, unless we empower ourselves with knowledge and support. Let's begin this journey by dispelling the misconceptions people have about autism.

19 Myths About Autism
Bill Davis

Myth #1: People with autism are incapable of loving.

Chris loves me with such passion. People with autism are angelic, loving human beings. The other day my wife Kate ordered some very cool sneakers for Chris. She called him over and presented him with his new, sharp, teenage shoes. Chris put them on and began to jump all around the house with a big smile on his face. He slowed down, looked up at Kate, and whispered, "I love you, Kate."

Myth #2: Everyone with autism is "Rainman" or a savant.

What is your child's skill? Autism is a spectrum disorder, a continuum of traits, gifts and strengths. I know people on the spectrum who have a Ph.D. and I know children on the spectrum who have Downs Syndrome. I have friends with autism who are married, as well as those who are embroiled in a terrific struggle with daily life, so everyone with autism is not "Rainman".

Myth #3: Autism affects life span.

People with autism do not die earlier than those who don't have autism. Most lead long, rich and fulfilling lives.

Myth #4: If your child with autism does not speak by a certain age, he will never speak.

My son, Chris, did not speak until age six. After age six, I asked him, "Hey Chris, what do you want to do tomorrow?" "I want to bath, I want to dress, and I want to go to Learning Center." Thanks for exploding that myth, Chris.

Myth #5: All people with autism want to be cured.

I know many people with autism who truly love and enjoy their lives. They don't feel they have a disorder, and simply think and exist on a different plane. They resent the word "cure." They are not diseased or broken, and thus do not need to be cured. I do believe in biomedical intervention and know recovered people, but a great portion of the population with autism is very happy the way they are.

Myth #6: People with autism do not develop friendships.

Untrue! My son has many friends. He relates to people on so many levels. Chris has maintained all types of relationships. Albeit, they may not be typical friendships, but he truly enjoys his pals. My son and I are good friends, and Chris and Kate have developed an outstanding relationship.

Myth #7: People with autism will never make eye contact.

Direct eye contact was very painful for Chris when he was young. He would catch glimpses of us by using his peripheral vision. One young man told me that he did not know what his mother's face looked like until he was ten! Eye contact can be overwhelming and facial expressions may be confusing, but eventually most of our kids will look right at us and smile.

Myth #8: Autism is a psychological disorder, although we treat it behaviorally.

Autism is not psychological. We now know that autism is a complicated developmental disorder. It may be genetically predisposed, and some believe triggered by environmental factors.

Myth #9: Bad parenting causes autism.

Do you remember the term, Refrigerator Mom? In the 1940s, psychologists decided that mothers of children with autism were so "cold" that they made their kids withdraw and develop strange behaviors with repetitive characteristics. Through the 1970s, because of this theory, mothers of children with autism suffered from blame, guilt and self-doubt, caused by the idea that their inadequate parenting caused the autism. Some children were actually placed with other "more responsive" families. They did not improve. Autism has nothing to do with parenting skills.

Myth #10: Autism is rare.

Most current estimates say that about one in a 110 children are diagnosed with autism. Autism is growing at alarming rates. Nearly everyone knows, or knows of a person with autism!

Myth #11: Nutrition, by itself, can cure autism.

Families have made tremendous strides utilizing the casein-free, gluten-free diet and other nutritional programs. Kids with autism tend to have digestive problems too, but nutrition is only one part of the puzzle.

Myth #12: Teaching social skills will develop social relationships.

Making friends can be tough for anyone, yet more difficult for people with developmental disorders. Kids and adults with autism do make friends, and we will discuss friendships for your child later in the book.

Myth #13: Before attempting a treatment, it must have research to back it up.

Our family has tried many therapies without clinical research behind them, and many proved valuable. Each child is unique.

Myth #14: People with autism are dangerous.

Most outbursts are due to pain, lack of communication, frustration or sensory overload. This is not a dangerous population.

Myth #15: People with autism do not smile.

The look on Chris' face when we take him to buy videos is one big smile!

Myth #16: People with autism will outgrow it.

Not true! Your child may appear to "normalize," but will always have autism.

Myth #17: People with autism don't want friends.

Not true! Ask your child.

Myth #18: People with autism cannot conceptualize.

Not true! Again, watch and ask your child.

Myth #19: People with autism do not have passion, energy, or emotion.

Not true! Kids with autism can be emotional, passionate and energetic!

10 Tips for Parents and Professionals to Promote Positive Relationships with Those on the Autism Spectrum
Karen Simmons

1. Understand the label: The label is not the problem as much as the fear of the unknown and preconceived notions with the label. We must first understand the challenges facing autism, then the communication and sensory challenges that result in social skill deficits and behavioral challenges. In addition, get past the label drama by offering people a better way to understand what's happening with your child. This ultimately supports differences and discourages discrimination.

People on the spectrum can be very literal, so don't take what they say personally. Look for things that may cause miscommunication, such as lighting and uncomfortable clothing. Understand your child's lack of inability to process and express themselves. Also, teach your child to balance themselves physically, emotionally, mentally, spiritually and intellectually.

2. Enhance empathy: Tune into empathy, not sympathy. Imagine what they may be thinking or feeling. They have difficulties expressing, understanding, and showing emotions, which makes the world confusing for you, them and others, but with interventions you can help.

3. Communication for community: Help to bridge relationships between peers and those with autism. This is an intuitive process, so be careful of boundaries. Try to help your child find a buddy to coach him. Get them to volunteer, sign up for an acting class or try to find others who have something in common. Building and fostering, nourishing, young relationships with peers, employers, family and community enhances the fabric of humanity.

4. Share the knowledge, by raising awareness and understanding of autism and the issues surrounding it: Typically, kids have issues around what is and what is not safe, and due to their literal nature, they are often seen as blunt and offensive. Educate peers, teachers, family and the community.

5. Remember learning styles: All people learn in different ways. Whether they process their world through sight, sound or touch determines the quality of their communication. Since many people with autism are generally visual learners and think in pictures, it is important to

11

communicate with pictures and words. You can find out how your child learns best by using the free Personal Learning Styles Inventory at www. HowToLearn.com

6. Scripting for success: If you want to communicate better, it is helpful to write the message. You can even use pictures to make your message easier to understand. This can be as simple as explaining the proper way to relate to friends, or writing a script for a movie or play.

7. Understand the "box." The "box" is the family unit surrounding the person with autism, a complete entity unto itself. Many times, people inside the "box" either go into denial or have spousal challenges. Those outside of the "box," such as teachers, in-laws, and others, who don't "live" it, may not understand the many family dynamics. Keep an open mind and treat both sides of the "box" equally.

8. Be a team player: While working together for the common goal of helping a person with autism build relationships, include parents, educators and professionals on the same page. It doesn't help the person if the support team can't agree. Always choose your battles carefully.

9. Empower people with autism to be who they are. Your child knows much more than you might imagine. Once you let go a bit, it can help your child build self-esteem, while they learn to be as independent as possible.

10. Autism is all about your child, and it is critical you know it is not about your ego, personality or lack of understanding. Never lose sight that your child is the focus of attention. Don't be afraid of what these special children know; be afraid of what they don't know.

In the world of autism, there is always a beautiful tomorrow. With love, caring, and kindness, it is just around the corner.

Chapter 2

All in the Autism Family

Chapter 2
All in the Autism Family

Mother's Issues

Here is a bit of folklore about an American Indian mother, which reminds me about all mothers who have a child with autism.

Her tribe lived at the bottom of a mountain. Another tribe dwelled atop the jagged peaks. One day the members of the second tribe scurried down the mountain and stole the mother's newborn child. She alerted the braves who attempted in vain to scale the rough and icy peaks. They collapsed at the campsite, bleeding and exhausted. Suddenly the Indian woman came scurrying down from the mountain, clutching her baby. The chief asked in amazement how she performed such a feat when even the strongest braves had failed. "They were not the mother," she replied.

...just as our families must adjust to the needs of those with autism, so must society...

—Gail Stein

Mothers are strong, resilient, and able to manage enormous stress. They bond with their children who have autism and delicately balance many roles.

Sometimes, moms feel they can never do enough. They must constantly consider new therapies, biomedical issues, diets and supplements, as well as attend conferences and understand educational law. The list is endless. They feel like they will never catch up.

Note: My first wife Jae passed away, all the while being the strongest mom possible. She suffered a painful, horrific battle with cervical cancer. Jae desperately continued to try to take care of the kids, never even taking time to consider her own well-being.

Since all our children are different, you may find that you are not doing what others are doing. Just follow your instincts. Once your child is diagnosed, you may find yourself alone. Moms can feel terribly isolated. Birthday party invitations sometimes 'evaporate', and it may be very difficult for your family during the holidays. Sadly, you may not get an invitation as often as you'd like to your friends' or families' homes for the holidays.

One time we visited a relative's home for a holiday and Chris ate mud in the back yard. That's when I learned about pica. Children with pica may eat animal feces, clay, dirt, hair balls, paint, or sand. If your child eats these, or any other odd items, be sure to check with your doctor and ask about pica. You may also want to have your child tested for nutrient deficiencies and lead exposure. The federal laws are changing drastically about lead and you need to know that, even your floor may contain lead, so get it tested, for your child's safety. There is some new Environmental Protection Agency (EPA) information on this subject, which you may want to research. You may also want to buy a home testing kit at stores like Home Depot, to test the areas in your home for anything that can negatively affect your family.

Parent Tip: Seek out friends or join a support group. Do not allow you or your family to become socially isolated.

Moms will often worry about finances. Suddenly, it may seem like you have no money for luxuries like hair appointments, manicures or the health club. It's a good idea to be good to yourself, and not feel guilty about it. You must start making time for your own medical appointments. Go to the gym. Make time for that romantic dinner you have been putting off. Take care of yourself emotionally, physically, and spiritually. Do not make the mistake that my wife Jae made. You cannot help your child if you are not around.

Mothers are often the ones who give up careers and stay at home. It's easy to forego education and you may lose touch with your friends, because taking care of a child with autism is such a tremendous responsibility. Moms very often give up their dreams and embrace a completely new lifestyle. Typical moms buy school clothes, pencils, make lunch, and send their children off to school. Mothers who have kids with autism attend meetings at school to create and help with their child's IEP (Individualized Education Program). You are your child's voice.

We hear a lot about children who are cured. Not all our children will respond as well as others. Do not second-guess yourself and do not look for the magic bullet. Concentrate on your own child and what is best for her.

Do not stress over the dreams you had for your child. We all have them. Your expectations will change. That does not mean you lower them. You may have to adjust them a bit. Look at Dr. Stephen Shore, a contributor to this book. His parents never gave up and neither did Stephen. Today, he is an extremely successful author, speaker, professor, and a witty, loving friend.

One thing I've seen a lot of is that moms tend to blame themselves when their child has autism. They believe they may have caused it in any number of ways, including genetically. Try to remember that your child gets his sweet natured heart, loving ways, and the ability to survive and thrive from you, and it won't serve anyone to worry about genetics. Also, know you're doing your very best, so don't fret over the endless therapies you've not tried yet either.

I know these words may sound trite, but every parent lives them and, as a parent of a child with autism, I've been there too. Thankfully, today, we're focusing on all the positive things about our lives with Chris, and have long forgotten any concerns about whether we did something to cause his autism. We didn't.

Here are Some Suggestions for Moms

Seek support: Utilize the Disabilities Network and the special needs community. These groups have parents and professionals who have a real understanding of what you are experiencing. They have lived it, and can provide information and comfort. We highly recommend internet blogs like www.Autisable.com so you can stay in touch and stay informed.

Respite care: Do not hesitate to apply for help at home. Your local Mental Health and Mental Retardation (MHMR) and other agencies have funding set aside to provide respite care. A qualified caregiver will come to your home and attend to your child.

This will allow time for work, study, school and even a massage! If you have a friend or family member who is interested in the job, they must obtain certification for home care education. Once that's in place, if insurance allows, have a home care agency hire the accredited person. The agency is happy because your insurance company pays it, your friend is paid an hourly rate, and you get some much-needed rest! When interviewing a caregiver you don't know, get references, watch them interact with your child and go with your instincts.

Seek professional help: Psychologists, psychiatrists, counselors, and social workers will help you cope with finances, stress and your journey through the world of autism. You may also benefit from a marriage counselor's advice. You may want to seek out a local Defeat Autism Now (DAN) doctor. He or she will suggest diet and supplements which may help your child significantly.

Take up writing: Recording your trials and tribulations can be very cathartic. It can also serve as a record for the IEP, mediation, or due process. If you are dedicated and inspired, you may end up writing a book!

Try advocating: Spreading awareness will provide you with great purpose. Advocating will help your child and others, empower you and change your life.

Enjoy your child to the fullest: Autism does not define your child. Go to the park, and enjoy each other. It is very hard not to make your child the center of your universe. When he becomes the sole driving force in your life, it is a cocoon-like existence. Don't make that mistake because it can limit your child. Your child needs independence.

Parent Tip: Moms, you have a wonderful life ahead of you. Children with autism are angelic. Your days will be filled with humor, drama, and love. You will change forever.

Father's Issues

Parent Tip: Fathers need to learn to persevere without ego. Take a stand based on your child's needs. It is more exciting to win something for your child on an Individualized Education Program (IEP) than a football game.

Be a dad first: Hug, wrestle, swim, joke and hike, but on your child's terms, and in his world. As Stephen Shore advised someone many years ago, "Just flap, flap and flap!"

Empower yourself: Study state regulations and educational law. Knowledge is power.

Please take the time to recognize the beauty of your relationship with your child. It may appear to be different, and it may be difficult to accept, but embrace it. Life will take on extraordinary beauty, and you will gain a sense of pride, better than you ever felt before.

Seek the advice of fathers with disabled children: Chat and compare notes. Those conversations can be very enlightening. Vent and ask these guys questions. You will develop a support group that you can count on.

Take an active role: Walk the walk. Visit your child's classroom, attend seminars, and be a part of his therapy. You'll learn so much about your child by speaking with his teachers, and at the same time, you can point out many of your child's nuances to them.

Here comes the biggest lesson dads have to learn. You are no longer the center of attention! The focus is not on you. Romance often dwindles and your dinner might be fast food, because your child requires a lot of time and attention.

I remember trying to wake Jae up one night to be romantic. She was sleeping soundly and did not respond at all. I walked over to the kitchen table in a huff. There were stacks of recorded data, sample IEPs, lesson plans and schedules. I learned very quickly that I was no longer the center of attention.

Stay strong and stay with your family. It is very clear that an absentee father cannot provide love or emotional strength.

> **Parent Tip**: Work as a family. You and your wife's methods and ideas may be different, so take time to recognize the validity of both.

Celebrate any small signs of progress. Chris took many "baby steps" to get to where he is now. Show your child that you are proud of his accomplishments.

Talk to your child. He may be non-verbal and appear inattentive, but notices the sound of your voice, as well as your emotions.

Give your wife a few days vacation, away from home. You may want to give her a spa day at a resort, some shopping days, or a few days travel, just so she can relax and forget the responsibilities at home. She'll return refreshed!

Moms, this next section is for you. We put together some tips that will help you improve your relationship with your husband.

Somewhere in your home, set up a table, complete with information that you want your spouse to read and review. Highlight important points and cut out articles. Keep him informed and involved. After winding down from a day's work, your husband can catch up on the world of autism.

Recognize the source of any conflict. Men are constantly concerned with monetary issues, the uncertainty of the future, and transitioning their child to adulthood. Tell him you understand his fears and frustrations.

Karen's Comments:

For me, my husband, Jim's lack of participation was very challenging. I felt so all alone because he was generally in denial about Jonny's diagnosis until Jonny was 14. One day Jim took Jonny to work with him and when they got home, Jim asked, "Did you know that all he does all day is sit in a corner and read?"

"Where have you been for the past 11 years, Sweetie?" I replied. I love Jim dearly and am thankful he now realizes more about, and is beginning to understand autism. I must say, in some ways, I have Jenny McCarthy, the gorgeous actress, to thank. She is happy, has REALLY helped our community, and the men pay attention. She wrote two books about her child's autism, and again, Jenny, thank you for helping me and so many other families who have a child with autism.

Siblings

Millions of American children have siblings with disabilities. More often than not, the typical siblings are pushed to the side, neglected or expected to act like adults. We put a lot of pressure on these brothers and sisters. We need to take the time to recognize the important role they play.

Comments from Bill Davis:

Here are some red flags to watch for in your other siblings:

Internalization and self-blame, helpless feelings, cutting/self-mutilation, change in sleeping habits, lack of concentration, skipping school, stomach pains or headaches, irritability, isolates self from others.

Here are Some Tips for Dealing with Siblings of Children with Autism That We've Learned

Please seek professional help. Demonstrate to the sibling how exceptional their brother or sister is. Lavish them with praise. Let them know that the sacrifices they are making are not only unselfish, but also very necessary.

Consider the age of the sibling when explaining the disorder. Adjust your explanation according to the level of comprehension. During family meetings, allow the sibling to express negative feelings.

Keep "in touch" with the sibling, no matter how demanding life with autism becomes. Remain understanding and accessible. Schedule some private time.

Offer honest and factual information and send the older sibling to a beginner's conference to enhance empathy.

Give them time to be a kid. Provide a place where siblings can keep their valuables or special things safe, so no one touches them.

Ensure your other children feel you honor them fairly, especially when your child with autism does something to them or their things, and isn't punished.

Finally, don't require your other children to modify their lives too much. Think about speaking to your other children's classmates. Explain autism and some of the sacrifices your typical children make. Hopefully, they will come away with an understanding of the disorder, and an appreciation of your child with autism.

Your home life may be very tense. You may have to keep the noise down and the lights low. Friends of your other siblings can't stay long. You may not be able to eat in front of your child because of his issues with food smells, and eating noises, so explain all of this to your child's siblings.

Please tell all your children you love them. At the same time, point out the beauty of their brother or sister with autism. Do not wait!

Karen's Comments

Thank God for siblings. I personally think they are the saving grace we need for our special needs kids! Long after my husband and I are gone, our special needs kids will have their siblings by their side.

In my home, my children will not tolerate abuse towards Jonny and Alex, and they stand strong for them. They are REAL with them, and empower them to move through their "stuff" in a safe environment. Just think of how much our special needs kids give to their siblings. They provide opportunities to develop compassion, patience, nurturing, and empathy they might not otherwise learn.

Here's an idea for you: Ask your other children the questions below and listen carefully to the answers to learn what they are thinking and feeling. This is especially important if your child with autism requires a great deal of your time and energy.

When I asked my children, Kimberly, Matthew, Christina, Stephen and Alex these questions about Jonny, for the most part, they felt okay with my son's autism and all would defend him to the end, in any circumstance. A couple of kids indicated they did feel left out sometimes, and were concerned about my son's weight gain (due to medication he'd taken) and his personal hygiene. Other than that, they felt that Jonny did not have a disorder at all.

Questions To Ask Your Child's Siblings

Do you ever feel neglected because of your sibling's disorder?

When you were younger, did you think your sibling could have just stopped doing certain behaviors, if he just wanted to?

How has it generally affected your life until you moved out? On the other hand, if you're still at home, how does it affect your life now?

What specific things do you remember most about your brother or sister with autism when you were younger?

Are you hesitant to bring friends home after school?

What kinds of things does your brother or sister with autism do that make you angry and upset?

What kinds of things does your sibling with autism do that literally make you feel grossed out?

How do you handle being the other kid when both parents have to step in and rescue your sibling with autism, when difficult things happen?

What do you notice about how autism affects your parents?

Which of your sibling's behaviors are most difficult for you?

How does your sister or brother's behavior affect you? Do you ever wish he would behave differently?

Do you ever do your own research, maybe on the Internet, to learn more about autism? If so, what did you learn that helped you?

Did you keep it "secret" from friends and classmates that your sibling has autism? If you did, why? If you told people, what did you tell them and how did they react?

Did you ever worry that this was hereditary, and that when you have children, they might have autism?

If you had to describe the best memory of how your sibling's disorder affected you and the family, what would it be?

What are some gifts and strengths your sibling brings to your life?

Extended Family and Friends
Karen Simmons

When a child is diagnosed with autism, it is incredibly important that all of the significant other people in the child's life completely accept, understand, and embrace autism, regardless of how difficult it may seem. This is truly for the benefit of all concerned so that the best and most effective interventions are fully integrated into your child's life.

Parent Tip: Acceptance and admission of the truth is the first step to set the family in motion for the best possible outcome.

The extended family feels a tremendous amount of stress. They want to help but have not developed skills to deal with your child's behaviors. They have no training. Sometimes your relatives cannot physically handle your child.

Some grandparents develop a fear of their grandchild. If they are alone with your child, they might be afraid of things like an outburst, running away, or not know how to understand what your child says, needs or wants. Sadly, this can mean that the grandparents stop coming to your home, and may want you to stop coming to theirs.

However, here are several tips to help your child's grandparents understand just how important your child is to them, and they are to your child.

Grandparents

Your parents may appear awkward around their grandchild with autism. They might be in a state of disbelief, seem unyielding, uneducated or perhaps even unkind. You need to realize that they are hurting too.

They longed for and expected the perfect little grandchild. They are grieving just like you. Your parents hurt for you because they see what you are going through. They would love to help, but without training and understanding, it becomes a very frustrating situation for them. If your parents are older, it may be physically impossible for them to handle your child.

Here Are Some Tips For Making Life Easier For Your Child's Grandparents

First, present an opportunity for them to attend conferences and trainings. If you have respite care, spend some quality time with your parents. It will do you both good.

Do not let your parents become frustrated. Explain how to communicate, how to handle outbursts, and how to play with their grandchild. They can even spoil their grandchildren if they are willing to learn the fundamentals of autism. Try to be patient with them.

Recommend a support group for the grandparents. If getting around is a problem, steer them to an online support group. Give them books and articles. Highlight the parts that you feel will directly relate to them.

Take them out for a special day with the grandkids. An enjoyable time might change their minds about your child's temperament.

What about giving grandparents information on the basics of autism? The www.AutismToday.com website is a wonderful place to begin. It provides insight into the disorder and allows you to ask our resident experts any questions. In addition, grandparents will enjoy the stories, poems, news and on-line conferences.

Explain the stress that is gripping your household, outline the financial burden you are facing and detail the schedule you follow day in and day out. Be honest about what to expect from the outside world. You need to let grandparents know, in advance, that their beloved grandchild might get stares or ridicule. Strangers may chastise you for not disciplining your child. Grandparents should expect to rearrange their homes in preparation for your visits. They must learn to lock doors and cabinets, be ready to put an unfriendly pet outside, provide quiet areas, and buy certain types of foods.

Tell grandparents why you are exhausted, tired and cranky. Let them know that they may feel slightly uncomfortable around your child for the first few visits. Keep communication open.

More Tips For Grandparents

Praise your grandchild constantly. Be very patient. Make your grandchild feel welcome, safe, and very loved. Understand and respect the seemingly strange things he does. Attempt to get into his world. Do not be condescending. Do not ridicule. Do not compare him to the typical grandchild. Do not be afraid to ask questions. Spoil him a little and love him a lot.

Friends and Your Child
Bill Davis

We all long for friendship. It appears to be inherent. Do you wrestle with the question of friendships and your child? We can help, but we also have to allow for a natural progression. A recluse is fascinating to us. A quirky loner

24

can be a genius. Some people may consider your child socially unacceptable however. Many of our kids are perfectly content not having friends, and do not feel lonely. Others desire relationships, but don't know how to go about securing one. Some feel isolated, but do not associate loneliness with not having friends.

Karen's Comment: My son Jonny considers his siblings his best friends.

Here is Some Advice to Help Your Children Approach and Secure Friendships

Find children who function on the same level as yours does. They should possess the same level of social activity. Shared interests help to form a bond. Computers, film, painting and music seem to be a common thread.

Friends should live in close proximity because travel can be difficult. Age is an important variable. Children closer in age seem to get along better.

If your child is befriending someone at the other end of the spectrum, again look for the same interests. If the groups of friends are higher functioning, make sure that they are warm, kind. You do not want a higher functioning child trying to control your child with more severe autism.

Arrange meetings with friends after school. If you are willing to provide transportation or suggest activities, it will be easier for your child to find a buddy. Contact the prospective friend's parents and make sure that everyone is on the same page, working towards the same goal.

Teachers can be of great help. Ask for a buddy system. Try to pair up a child with autism with a 'neurotypical' (normal child) peer. They can work on projects together. The typical friend can watch out for your child, and they learn from each other. Teach and use social stories to define and describe friendship. These tools can help a child with autism recognize bullying. It is not the magic bullet, but has its place. Video modeling can help or just watching a movie about friends interacting kindly will prove a great aid. Teachers should talk to the parents and try to bring children together. The family must always play a major and reassuring part. "Autism is a way of being," says Jim Sinclair, a high-functioning autism activist who formed the Autism Network Intervention. Friendships may prove difficult, but if successful, extremely rewarding.

Here Are Some Difficulties Your Child Might Encounter While Hanging Out with His Friends

Children with autism have difficulty reading body language. It is very hard to be social when you don't understand how.

Your child must learn to maintain proper body space. Standing too close, improper touching, or touching oneself is easily misunderstood. Talk to your child about this subject early and often.

Kids with autism sometimes speak in a monotone or robotic-like voice. This can be very disconcerting to a social group.

Some of our kids do not maintain proper speaking volume. They talk very loudly or blurt out some very honest comments. Sometimes this can be very charming, but it can also interfere when developing friendships.

Once you help your child manage these issues, using social stories or videos, your child will find it easier to be around friends.

Information for Those Who Work with Your Child
Bill Davis

Our children are as special to us as yours are to you. Even though they may act differently, and aren't as understood as well as we'd hope, they are still a valuable contribution to our world.

Caretakers or others who work with your child may appear that they don't really care about your child, but they do. Please be sensitive and make every effort to understand what they are thinking and feeling.

Anticipate their needs and help them to learn and grow, so they will fit into your child's world, just as we fit into theirs.

Help caretakers to understand what your child must do to make friends. For our kids, it is more difficult because they don't typically seek out friendships.

Give some advice to the caretaker, to help bridge the gap between home and any other environment.

Try to explain autism and the signs of autism to everyone.

Do this especially with the potential friends of the child with autism, by telling them that some things a child with autism does may appear odd, or that the child with autism really does care, but that they just have a slightly different way of showing their feelings.

Parent Tip: Everyone expects high-functioning kids with autism to act and behave like the next guy, when they are not like the next guy!

Pets are Important
Bill Davis

Kids with autism can benefit a great deal from having pets. Pets seem to operate on a different wavelength, and kids with autism seem to be somewhat intuitive with them.

How Dogs Help Kids with Autism

- Can reduce anger
- Can comfort your child
- Will always play with their companion
- Your child will focus on the dog instead of stressful stimuli
- The dog provides safety
- Dogs make trips more enjoyable
- Dogs have extraordinary patience
- Dogs teach kids responsibility

Dogs help many non-verbal children navigate their world, and become much more independent. The dogs actually watch out for the children, just as they do for those challenged by the lack of sight, hearing or mobility. Cats can also be good for children with autism. In fact there is even a book entitled, *All Cats have Asperger's*, which alludes to fact that they're like those on the spectrum, because they are aloof, egocentric, selective and so on.

Please remember that the dog must fit the child, because each child is unique. It costs about $45,000 to train a companion dog and most parents utilize donations and private grants. The company itself may get grants so they can donate dogs to families who qualify. However, some agencies ask families to pay as much as $20,000 for a companion dog, so do your homework before paying for a dog you may be able to get at no cost. That said, here are some helpful sites where you can get companion dogs, and again, you'll want to look at all your options.

Canine Companions for Independence – www.caninecompanions.org

The Guiding Eyes Site - www.guidingeyes.org

North Star Dogs - www.northstardogs.com (funded 100% by donations to the site)

Autism Service Dogs of America - www.autismservicedogsofamerica.com

Talk to other parents, educators, and providers for more information on funding a companion dog for your child.

Holidays and Other Special Days

Holidays can be very rough for the family with autism. Visiting relatives, and the anticipation of gifts, can all translate into stress for the child with autism. Change and holidays go together. Your child's schedule is thrown off. You ask your child to wear special outfits, and be on his best behavior. Well-meaning relatives will overwhelm him with a barrage of kisses, pinches, smells, lights or noise.

Holiday Tips

Use social stories (see more detail in Chapter 7: Tools for the Outside World, to help). Explain exactly what will take place during the holidays.

Make sure you give your child a form of communication to indicate the need for a break. Tell your relatives that they must provide your child with a "quiet room." A TV and VCR or DVD player will usually make your child happy. Bring things that comfort your child. Try to keep your usual routine intact. Try not to show stress during the holidays. When you show anxiety, your child will notice it big time. Don't strive for perfection.

Marriage and Divorce
Bill Davis

In a Detroit Free Press article about autism, Dr. Colleen Allen, Director of the Henry Ford Center for Autism and Developmental Disabilities said, "More often than not, it rips apart marriages. Eighty-six percent of the marriages with an autistic child end in divorce." Other articles state reasons such as guilt, fear, ego, financial implications and even blame.

Autism will always be a strain on your marriage. Even a very strong relationship can succumb to the demands of autism. Some families learn to embrace it. Some become stronger, but many divorce. Divorce rates are skyrocketing for parents of children with autism. Both spouses feel isolated. There are communication problems and a constant fight for attention.

Most children diagnosed with autism are male, and the male role model is critical for our children. That said, most primary caregivers are female, so we know we need more resources in the relationship area to help parents work through the challenges and take on a united front.

Divorce is very difficult for our children. They have a great fear of the unknown and may be incapable of expressing their fear and anger. Seek professional help. Finding social workers and marriage counselors who are familiar with the disorder can be very comforting.

Tips if You Are Divorcing

If you are divorcing or separating, do not allow the situation at home to become too intense. Gear your talks to the child's level of understanding. Keep it simple, clear and concise. Don't blame your spouse. Discuss new schedules. Explain meeting Dad or Mom at a new place. Use visual schedules. Use social stories to explain marriage and divorce.

The National Autism Association perceives divorce as such a problem, that it has launched the first national program to combat divorce rates in the autism community.

Tips to Keep Your Marriage Strong and Stable

- Do not play the blame game. The mother often gets the blame for what she may have consumed during the pregnancy. Keep lines of communication open. Both of you should be on the same page, especially where treatment is concerned.

- Understand that one or the other parent may be in denial about their child's autism diagnosis.

- Do your best not to assume that one or the other of you has a predisposition link which caused the autism.

- Take time to understand your partner's needs. Give a little. Learn the fine art of compromise.

- Spend time alone and don't feel guilty. Solitude is not only good for your soul, it's good for your marriage.

- Schedule a date, an interlude or a romantic dinner. Autism is all consuming, bogging us down with meetings, research and conferences. We married because we loved each other's company, and now have very little time together. Do your best to create as much time together as you can.

- If you have a culturally different marriage, your belief systems may be challenging. Sometimes, the autism diagnosis itself causes family ties to break down. Learn as much as you can, and share this with both families.

- Insist that you and your spouse schedule regular physical checkups. You both need great health to handle your child's disorder, so don't compromise this.

- Reach out to the special needs community. Find comfort and support with other couples. Exercise together. Purchase a family health club membership.

- Married couples often experience waves of frustration and pain. Communication problems may arise, and the feelings toward the child might be differnent for the mother and the father. It's best to work towards a joint approach and acceptance of your child's diagnosis. Cooperative parenting is the key to a better outcome for your child's future.

- Your child will see many, many specialists. Follow the same course to help your marriage. See psychiatrists and counselors to develop communication strategies and coping skills.

Parent Tip: Remember the three 'Rs'. Respect your partner. Refresh your relationship. Renew your vows.

Chapter 3

Teaching
Acceptance and Understanding

Chapter 3
Teaching Acceptance and Understanding

Many parents suffer through five stages of grief after receiving the autism diagnosis for their child. These stages are outlined the magnificent book, *On Death And Dying* by *Dr. Elisabeth Kübler-Ross,* and this chapter helps you through each stage.

...we live in a society where acceptance is achievable through respectful means
—Donna Williams

Denial: When you first hear that your child has autism, you may be in deep denial. "This isn't happening to me!" Fathers seem to remain in this phase of suffering longer than mothers and most fathers I know do not accept the diagnosis quickly. They tend not discuss or speak of their child's diagnosis. From one father to another, I need to say that you must move on, because autism is not a death sentence and you have a child to care for and love.

Anger: We all envision a perfect little baby. When that baby isn't what we expect, we feel angry. It turns our lives upside down. Everything we planned changed. I lived this first hand and more than empathize. However, the rage eventually dissipates, and you will move on.

Bargaining: Bargaining is akin to guilt. Basically, we try and bargain our way out of the pain by asking if things will change if we are a better person. We all suffer greatly during this stage of grief. We wonder if we did something to cause this or ask if we are doing enough for our child. We feel twinges of guilt if we take time out for ourselves, if we spend money on ourselves, or spend quality time with other members of our family. Why haven't we cured our child? Are we utilizing every resource available? We feel so guilty in the beginning. Take one step at a time and choose what works for your child.

Slowly gather information and use your intuition. Take a deep breath and do something nice for yourself today because it moves you through this phase a little more quickly.

Depression: In this phase, we tend to develop an intense fear of the future. Overload sets in with so much to digest and very often, we get depressed because we don't have all the answers right now. You'll have big questions during this time, which affect your child's future. For example, you might wonder what are the first and best steps to take. You may experience depression and fear when you see how much new information you have to learn. You'll want to determine how to provide financial security immediately, and question where your child will live after you die. The diagnosis feels like a swift punch to the gut. All the "unknowns" cause great trepidation and fear.

The best advice is to empower yourself. Knowledge of the disorder helps eradicate your fears, and ease the depression. Take things in slowly. Study educational law, which is true empowerment. Surround yourself with good friends, loving family members and a strong, knowledgeable support group. Seek professional help if you feel yourself sinking into despair.

Acceptance: We finally come to terms with the diagnosis. Autism will always be a major part of our lives. We will live it every day. You must take this journey together with your child. If you are married, try to meet each other's needs. Work as one to overcome any stereotypical views you may have of this disorder. We may want our child to recover or become high functioning and of course, there are very severe cases of autism. However, with knowledge, kindness, and love your child will keep growing. Early intervention is the first thing you want to learn more about on your way to true acceptance and love of your child.

Parent Tip: Stay calm. Empower yourself, your spouse, and your children. Love the child with autism for who he is, and take time to love yourself a little, too.

Explaining Death and Grief

Karen's Comments: My son Jonny's best friend tragically died when a truck hit him. Jonny went to the funeral and all the kids released balloons to send to Mikey in the sky.

One day, without my knowledge, shortly after Mikey's death, Jonny took his two younger brothers, Stephen and Alex, then five and three, across a busy highway to find Mikey's grave in the cemetery.

This is a big issue with our kids: They seem have no concept of fear and safety. You'll read more about this when Bill talks about the brain, and why this may happen. Anyway, when Jonny and his brothers returned home safely, Jonny told me that he wished he could have unlimited lives, like in his computer game, so he could add a life for Mikey. Even though Jonathan didn't usually show his emotions, he did show that he missed Mikey terribly.

When your child experiences a friend or loved one's death, it's good to ask as many questions as possible. Whether you think they have feelings about death or not, assume they do, and do your best to calm their fears and answer all their questions. Make sure they are not planning a trip to the cemetery without you!

Bill's Comments

My wife, Jae, was sick for almost two years, and then passed away. At first, Chris was extraordinarily angry. He wanted his mom to play with him, take walks, and tickle him. I sat Chris down and very simply explained how sick she was, and when she died, that she would not be with us anymore.

I told him that he could hold on to Mommy in his heart. It seemed to comfort him. Social stories are a wonderful visual tool for explaining death. Thank God for Carol Gray, the developer of the social story concept!

Here Are Some Things About Death and the Grief Process We Learned from Several Sources

1. Once again, seek professional help. Attend grief counseling and get help for your other children as well. See if the school's guidance counselors and social workers can advise and console your child. Make sure your child with autism is cared for properly. This is very common because people do not recognize the heart and soul of the disabled, or are sometimes stumped, so they don't do anything.

2. Do not make unrealistic promises to yourself or your children.

3. Look into future care giving in case your spouse passes away. If you are a single parent, discuss this topic openly with siblings and other relatives.

4. Research and adjust trust funds, wills, living arrangements, job training, and medical care. (See more about this in Chapter 15)

5. Do not isolate yourself. Research some different ways to let any feelings of guilt melt away. Exercise, as this often improves your mood.

6. When you explain death to your child, use simple and appropriate language. Do not use abstract sayings that your child will likely perceive as literal, such as 'the angels took her' or 'she rode a chariot to heaven.' Be open and honest. Do not send mixed messages like "She is in a better place, or she is happier now." You child may interpret this as a death being their fault. Your child might ask why being with them wasn't a good enough place. Listen very careful to your child. Observe and proceed slowly. If your child asks questions, do not avoid them.

Despite your best intentions, your child may regress. Watch for bed-wetting or urinating in inappropriate places. He may shut down or lose language. Depression may take over and your child might internalize his anger. Stay very close and give a few extra hugs if your child likes them. You may need to seek professional help during this time so don't hesitate for a minute to do that, because a death may affect your child's overall development.

It's important for anyone in the autism community to understand that parents have the right to make time to express basic human emotions. If we do not allow for depression, sadness, loneliness, or grief, we will be incapable of taking care of our children properly. Do not jeopardize your health and well-being.

The Right Words

People are different, so one person might think a word is offensive, and another might not agree. Choose your words carefully and delete derogatory or demeaning words from your vocabulary. Many people believe it is important to say, "a person with autism" rather than "an autistic person," or "a person with sighting challenges" rather than a blind person. Karen came across this a great deal when writing the *Chicken Soup for the Soul: Children with Special Needs* book. If we treat each other with respect, love, and dignity and use the best language we know, all is well.

35

Chapter 4

Special Education and Transitions

Chapter 4
Special Education and Transitions

Individualized Education Program (IEP)
Bill Davis

I share the joys and challenges associated with life in the special needs sphere
—Jennifer Parsons

The centerpiece of the special education law is the Individualized Education Program (IEP). The IEP is a broad, intriguing, and complicated subject, and after some basics, we'll offer some tips we've learned over the years. As Keri Bowers mentions in the Epilogue, do your best to make this a collaborative, rather than a defensive process.

As the parent, you are an equal participant in the IEP process. You will provide valuable information to help plan your child's education. I've discovered that it's best when both parents attend; however, if this is not possible, you may want to bring an advocate or support person with you.

Your child's IEP must include comprehensive treatment programs. If you include Applied Behavioral Analysis (ABA) for example, it can help reduce behavioral problems and teach the child new skills. Behavioral interventions will encourage positive behaviors and can aid in coping strategies. They will help your child deal with change.

Items You Want on Your Child's IEP

Measurable Short and Long-Term Goals

After years as a special education expert, with both participant and administrative roles, Pat Wyman recommends that you ensure these goals be customized and specific to your child. Broad goals, such as, 'Your child will gain 5 months of reading fluency for 9 months of instruction' won't set your child up for success. If your child meets this goal, your child continues to fall behind; if not, you don't know why, or how to adjust the goal to facilitate your child's full potential. Put teaching methods on the IEP, along with how these methods are individualized to your child, and include how learning styles, sensory issues, communication and visual processing needs are met as well. Again, make sure this is all very specific. If you don't have this foundational information, it makes authentic measurement impossible and you cannot determine alternatives if your child is not making sufficient progress benchmarks to enable her to reach her goals.

Write the Names of Responsible Persons, Testing Conditions and Frequency of Assessments

As you formulate the IEP together with the team, Pat says to make sure to include the names of each person responsible for implementing the goals, along with the names of those responsible for fulfilling them if the primary person is absent or unavailable. Ensure a noise-free, distraction-free test setting if your child needs it, by placing this on the IEP. Include how often your child is tested, and how you are informed of your child's progress. Make this as specific as possible.

Request, in Writing, That You Tape Record Each IEP Meeting

Pat also recommends that you tape or audio record each IEP meeting, and notify the school, well in advance, that you will be taping all meetings. This tape ensures that you can share the information with your spouse if they aren't present, and serves to jog your memory at any time.

More Tips to Create the Highest Quality IEP

Meet with the principal, discuss your child's needs, and assure the teachers you are there to support them as well as your child. Take a close look at the school. Learn how far your child has to go to get to the bathroom, lunch room, etc. Determine "quiet areas" for your child.

Remember to request that your child's IEP list all of your child's strengths and needs. Evaluation methods must be very clear. It's not enough that you hear, "Your child waves good-bye 70% of the time, when prompted by peers." You need to know about the other 30% of the time. As a parent, you will want to include calming strategies and methods to relieve stress. Initiate a no-bullying policy on the IEP.

Include a number of methods that allow your child to transition from subject to subject. The IEP should contain a form of communication to indicate the need for a break or rest. Put in a detailed description of sensory and bathroom issues. This will be a comfort to your child.

Tips to Make the Transition to School Easier for Your Child

Drive your child to school for the first few days. Identify and introduce your child to all classroom, playground, lunchtime aides, custodians, school nurses and bus drivers. Practice sports, games, and exercise with your child so there are no surprises. Ask a 'neurotypical' child to buddy up with your child. They will both gain from the experience. Videotape the classroom and the hallways to familiarize your child with his school surroundings. If possible, have the teacher observe your child at home before the start of the school year.

Just as we did for Chris, tape words on playground equipment if you think this will help your child use it. Give the school office the same information you give emergency service providers. This includes contact numbers, allergies, sensory and behavioral issues, care providers, and how to communicate with your child.

Plan and rehearse arrival and dismissal times. Sometimes it works to get your child to school fifteen minutes after everybody and leave fifteen minutes before. This allows a smoother, quieter transition.

Use a daily communication book. Request specific information in this book. What did your child study today? Were there any glitches? What were the highlights of his day? You'll want to know more than your child had a nice day. Last bit of advice, stay positive, and focused on your child's needs.

Who is on the IEP Team?

You are the expert on your child and you will want to strive to form a good relationship with all the people guiding your child's education. You'll meet regular teachers, special education teachers, a school system representative, speech and language specialists, psychologists, occupational therapists, and more during an IEP. I always suggest bringing a child advocate with you to these meetings, as they can help decipher the legal language, and ensure the very best for your child.

Work towards positive outcomes, with collaboration in mind, and aim for a simple IEP document. A complicated document does not mean a more professional one. People working in harmony will create an intelligent plan for your child. If you ever feel tired during an IEP meeting, take a break. If you don't understand the list of abbreviations for educational terms, ask. Prior to starting the IEP meeting, it's a good idea to agree on communication etiquette and rules.

When you decide placement, you are aiming to make it the Least Restrictive Environment (LRE). Place your child with those who don't have disabilities as often as possible.

You are entitled to a copy of the IEP and all the rights that go with it. Before you sign your agreement, you may want to take the document home overnight and read it. You will be asked to sign that you attended the meeting, so now is a good time, if you disagree with the document in any way, to put in parenthesis, "Do not agree."

If you are really out of agreement, you are entitled to multiple legal venues to solve this problem. Seek an attorney's advice and again, do your best to realize that your child's special needs will be met.

Sometimes, school personnel may not follow all the goals on a signed IEP. At this point, they are out of compliance, so do your best to resolve this yourself, and if it doesn't get resolved, seek legal counsel here as well.

Resources

One of your best resources that we all highly recommend is Wrights Law at www.wrightslaw.com. Pete and Pam Wright are Adjunct Professors of Law at the William and Mary Law School where they teach a course about special education law and advocacy and assist with the Law School's Special Education Law Clinic. They are co-authors of several books published by Harbor House Law Press.

Parents, educators, advocates, and attorneys; go to www.Wrightslaw.com for accurate, reliable information about special education law, education law, and advocacy for children with disabilities.

In addition, a great resource for regulations, time constraints, and procedures is the National Dissemination Center for Children with Disabilities (NICHCY). Contact them at www.nichcy.org

Early, Middle, and Later Phases of Transition
Carolyn T. Bruey and Mary Beth Urban

Autism Today is proud to include this very powerful and practical information excerpted from *The Autism Transition Guide: Planning the Journey from School to Adult Life,* by Carolyn T. Bruey and Mary Beth Urban. Woodbine House published this book in 2009, and we highly recommend you pick up a copy at www.WoodbineHouse.com. Both authors provided written permission to excerpt and reprint the following sections, including the fill-in portfolio. We've omitted some of their sections, charts and tables in our book, so you'll want to get complete information with their book.

The transition goals during a student's school-age education must align with his or her life outcomes. It is important to note that later transitions require the student to move more quickly through each transition phase…

Keeping a Transition Portfolio

Keeping a paper trail for each area will be extremely beneficial… and a good way to keep everything organized is to use an accordion folder or a binder with two-pocket folders labeled with each of the areas of transition: 1) postsecondary education, 2) employment, 3) living arrangements, 4) community involvement, 5) leisure activities, and 6) interagency linkages. Transition-related documents to include in your portfolio are:

IEPs, results of assessments, applications for jobs and schools, resumes, emergency contact information, financial records, medical information, other paperwork that relates to each area of transition.

Organizing these documents for easy access is important. You may need this paperwork to support a change in services or for a new service after your child leaves high school.

During your child's school years, the educators and agency members can help you create this portfolio. Ensure, however, that you have access to and copies of all paperwork related to transition. You and/or your child will be responsible for maintaining the portfolio after your child leaves high school.

Early Phases of Transition Planning

The Individuals with Disabilities Education Act (IDEA) requires that transition planning begin at age 16, and some state laws mandate a starting age of 14. An ideal IEP program, planning for life outcomes beyond school, would begin as soon as the child enters elementary school. Unfortunately, most families are not ready to look that far ahead because they believe that would mean lowering expectations. That is not at all what it means! Targeting life outcomes can begin as early as kindergarten as long as we are looking at ways to teach a student to communicate, participate, solve problems, observe, read, and write.

Students with Autism Spectrum Disorders become eligible for specially designed instruction for a wide variety of reasons. Often, however, it is because they demonstrate deficits in the areas of expressive and receptive communication, social interaction skills, and repetitive or rigid interests and activities. Since this is a spectrum disorder, the needs of students and the programming to address the needs will vary in scope and intensity for every student.

In early phases of transition, teams are encouraged to begin where the student is. That is, it is helpful to assess the student's level of independence in expressive and receptive communication, in social interaction skills, and in activities of daily living. It is also useful to understand how the student's rigid interests and passions might affect her education. Developing or increasing your child's independence should be the primary goal in the early stages of transition. The team should also consider your child's rate of learning and her need for repetition, maintenance, and generalization of skills through each stage of the learning process. Only then can your child's team begin to consider if the vision that they have for her is realistic.

Middle Phases of Transition Planning

Depending on the student's age, teams may need to move quickly to the middle phases of transition. They may spend only a year or two in the early phases if transition planning began at age 16, assuming the student will continue in school beyond age 18 or 19. If a team started transition planning when the student was in middle school even prior to the age mandated by laws, the middle phase of transition could begin between the ages of 14 and 16. Typically, during the middle phase of transition planning, a student is either entering high school or has been there for a year or two.

During the middle phase of transition, you can begin to focus more specifically on life outcomes for your child. That is, what does the team want your child to know and be able to do once she leaves school? Life outcomes include living arrangements, employment or day-to-day activities, interaction in the community, and leisure activities. The IEP team will focus on the areas that the law requires for transition and begin to outline specifics for programming.

The questions are the same as in the early phases of transition; i.e. what is the focus area, is your child independent in that area, and who is the best person to help achieve the desired outcome? The IEP transition team can begin to define a comprehensive transition plan for the student with Autism Spectrum Disorders (ASD). In an ideal world, this phase of transition would begin when the student is 12 to 14 years old.

Why? Because in the United States today, the supports for transition stop once a student leaves high school. Beyond high school, there are no IEP transition teams mandated to continue the road map for the student. Moreover, for those parents who are looking at supported living and work opportunities for their child with ASD, there are simply not enough supports out there to meet the demand. Support systems created during the school years are what families have to continue supporting the student with after she leaves high school.

Considering Options for Post-Secondary Education

If your child with ASD heads in this direction, the team will want to ensure that she is on the academic path to graduation that will support entrance into a college or technical program. You and your child should work with guidance counselors to explore programs and supports that are available for students with disabilities. Students who do not have disabilities generally begin this process a year or two before high school graduation. For your child, it will probably make sense to begin earlier. You will probably need extra time to find a school or program that will be a good fit.

In our book, we provide an overview of the types of postsecondary schools that may be appropriate for students with autism spectrum disorders. If you or your child is unsure which of these types of programs might be best for her, here are some steps you might take:

Read books or directories targeted to students with learning disabilities who are considering college, arrange a visit to a program you are considering, speak to students with disabilities and their families about their experiences in a particular school or program (the school may be able to help you find alumni/students to talk with.)

Explore listservs or chatrooms on the Internet that focus on high functioning autism or Asperger's disorder where members talk about experiences related to postsecondary education. During the last two years of school, explore a dual-enrollment with a local college (if available) so that the student can explore options prior to graduation.

In addition to narrowing down what type of school or program your child might attend after high school, it will also be important to look into any testing that might be required as a prerequisite to attending the school.

Will your child be required to take the ACT or SAT to get into the college of her choice? If so, you need to request testing accommodations well in advance of the test and be prepared to supply documentation proving that your child needs accommodations. If your child tends to do poorly on standardized tests but still has potential to succeed in college, you might want to research the schools that do not require SAT/ACT tests for admittance. See www.FairTest.org under "University Testing" for a list.

Will your child need to provide IQ or achievement test scores to get into a program or to receive accommodations under Section 504? If so, how old can the scores be? Do you need to arrange for the high school to do particular evaluations of your child while he is still eligible for evaluations under IDEA? (Doing so can save you a great deal of money, as private evaluations can run into the thousands of dollars.)

Keeping in mind that a student with ASD can remain in public school until

45

age 21 or until she receives a high school diploma, the stakeholders will want to begin looking into postsecondary options as early as the student's first year in high school. To be highly prepared for postsecondary education, some students with ASD require a couple of extra years to complete both the general education requirements and their specially designed program within the IEP.

Considering Options for Employment

Assessments that are more specialized may be necessary to determine your child's present skill levels, as well as her aptitude for skill attainment. A Career Center, Office of Vocational Rehabilitation, or another rehabilitation service in your area may be a starting place for such an assessment. Bear in mind that there may be a waiting list to obtain an evaluation, so do not put this off too long.

The highly effective IEP transition team will work together to generate assessments appropriate for your child. For example, the team can begin assessing whether a student has the interest or skills to perform a particular job. Oftentimes, educators, occupational therapists, and job trainers can work together to research specific jobs and develop a task analysis of skills that are required to perform those skills. To do so, they will break down the skill into its component skills for easier teaching.

Your child's IEP team should write goals and objectives that will lead to your child developing needed work skills. Subsequently, job-training experiences can enable your child to learn and practice work skills in competitive and/or supported employment.

The middle phase of transition is a time to try out different types of employment. The IEP can incorporate job experience into your child's school day. These experiences could be within the school setting or at a nearby community agency or business. Some students may find it beneficial to get part-time jobs if they are old enough to do so. The IEP team needs to determine what is best for each individual child based on the data provided by observations and assessments.

If the student still needs to work on prerequisite skills required for specific jobs, the teacher and job coach should work to design tasks that will build these skills. For example, if a student wants a clerical position but is a slow typist, build time into the school day for the student to improve this skill. If, however, this same student is unable, even with assistive technology, to perform the keyboarding skills required of a clerical support person, the educational team and vocational agency staff should use the data they glean from working with the student to discuss other employment options. Perhaps the student could answer phones and take messages or greet guests who enter an office.

Considering Options for Living Arrangements

There are various types of living arrangements to consider for your child with an ASD as she approaches her adult years. Each type of arrangement provides a different amount of support.

Home-based services: Using this option, your adult child can continue to live in your home but receive services that free parents and other family members from some care giving responsibilities (and may teach the adult with ASD needed skills) These services are provided by trained staff in the family home. Support areas include personal care, medical appointments, and grocery shopping.

Supported living: In this arrangement, the adult with an ASD lives in her own apartment or other residence. She receives individual supports in her own home based on her specific needs. Types of supports may include assistance with budgeting, meal planning, transportation, and medical appointments.

Life sharing: In this type of arrangement, a family, well matched to the individual, provides a home, companionship, and needed support for the adult with an ASD. Family members receive training to support the individual so that she can meet her needs and achieve life goals.

Community homes, also known as group homes: These provide a home and staff who assist each person with personal, social, and physical activities for up to twenty-four hours a day.

Parents and guardians, if you have any notion that your child may require any type of assisted living as an adult should work with agency personnel to get on the list. Some areas are reporting as much as a ten-year waiting list for group home living. It is better to search out living arrangement options and complete applications that you may later determine are not necessary than it is to wait until closer to graduation time to begin your quest.

While researching available options, the team must begin to plan for increasing your child's independent living skills. During the middle phase of transition, it is important to consider:

The activities of daily living addressed in the early phase of transition as well as any new grooming or hygiene skills connected with entering adolescence or adulthood; your child's ability to feed herself and to purchase and prepare food; your child's ability to manage finances and health care.

How Much Do You Do for Your Child?

This is a good time for you, the parent, to make a list of all that you do for your child with ASD during the day. Write down everything—from waking her in the morning to reminding her to brush her teeth--for a period of two weeks to a month. You don't want to forget making appointments for haircuts and the dentist! Then, use the list to determine what you do for your child out of habit that she may be capable of doing herself. These are skills that you can give her to encourage responsibility.

Talk with your child to determine where to start and what she needs to complete each task. Also, communicate with the school team to determine how your child could practice the skill at school, if appropriate. School personnel can also assist you with task analyses of skills if you are having trouble teaching them at home.

Interagency Involvement

There is a lot to do to prepare a student with ASD for life after graduation. Don't expect to single-handedly prepare the student. Agencies bring a unique perspective to the team because they can assist with bridging the gap between school-age supports and post-graduation supports. Agencies can be very helpful in assisting with living arrangements and employment opportunities, not to mention exploring respite care facilities. They can also help families obtain funding.

Later Phases of Transition Planning

As with the early and middle phases of transition, this phase may begin earlier for some students than for others. The latest time to move into this phase is during the last two to three years of a teenager's time in school. This means that if an IEP team got a later start on transition planning, the team may need to combine some of the aspects of the middle phase with this later phase of transition. If you are in this situation, don't panic! It is easy to combine the two phases. It just means more work in a shorter amount of time.

The goals during the later phase of transition should center on narrowing the focus of programming to make sure that your child gains the skills she needs to move seamlessly from high school to adult life. The IEP goals should incorporate her needs related to postsecondary education and/or employment, living arrangements and activities of daily living, community involvement, and leisure activities. In the most seamless transition plan, your child's final year of high school would involve her spending a portion of the day at school and another portion of the day in the setting that she will participate in after leaving high school.

Easing Your Child into Adult Life

It is difficult for anyone to navigate multiple changes at one time. If a student with an autism spectrum disorder experiences too many changes too quickly, she may develop anxiety issues or shut down and fail. Introduce changes that will take effect after leaving high school one at a time over a long period. For example, don't ask your child to move out of your home, and start a job simultaneously. Also, students with ASD should be given as much time as they need in order to adjust to each change before being presented with another.

It is critical to start moving from school to life outcomes during the last two years of school. For example, once the type of employment is determined, your child should spend at least a portion of the week in that setting performing the work tasks. As she gets closer to leaving high school, she should ideally be spending full weeks in the new setting while supports from the school are faded. This provides a seamless transition from school to work. Similarly, your family and agency personnel can work with your child to become more involved in community leisure activities during the last two years of school. Then, as the final semester approaches, you can begin to plan for summer activities outside of the school setting.

Sometimes it is difficult to create a seamless transition from school to work or postsecondary education. In those situations, the IEP team must develop a program that helps to simulate the post-school activities to the best of their ability, using whatever resources are available. For example, providing a student with community-based instruction opportunities is critical to help prepare her for the differences between high school and college. If a student is going to eat in a cafeteria at college, the student could go to different buildings (businesses, hospitals, schools, etc.) that have cafeterias to learn to order and pay for meals in a cafeteria setting.

Teams will need to "think outside the box" to create opportunities for the student to try out activities that will prepare her for life after school. For example, if a student is planning to move into an apartment or group home and has never had a roommate, she could go to a sleepover camp to experience sharing a room with a stranger. The key aspect of using a similar experience is that the student will require a coach or instructor to help her understand how to apply the similar experience to the ultimate real experience. Otherwise, the literal-thinking person with ASD potentially will have a harder time adjusting to life after high school.

Staying Receptive to Change

Flexibility is the key to surviving each phase of transition. Remember, once your child leaves the public school system, she will no longer be eligible for transition services and supports under IDEA. Your child's eligibility for special education will stop when she: 1) graduates from high school with a diploma, or 2) reaches age 21. Before you and your child decide that she should leave the public school system, you should carefully balance the pros and cons:

If the goal is for your child to attend a postsecondary institution such as college, technical school, or a postsecondary program for students with disabilities: Does she need remedial work in any classes before she handles regular coursework at the college? What are the advantages of her doing the remedial work at the college vs. spending an extra year in high school doing the work?

Even if your child is academically qualified to go to college, would she benefit from more time in high school learning social skills or daily living skills that would help her succeed in a college environment? Is your child unwilling to stay in high school after her classmates graduate? Is it to your family's financial advantage for your child to remain in high school an extra year or two? (e.g., more time to save money for college tuition; issues related to eligibility for government benefits).

If the goal is for your child to begin a job immediately after leaving high school: Does your child have the social, motor, communication, transportation, or other skills needed to succeed in the type of job she prefers? Could she continue to develop these through therapies, coaching, etc. at school if she remained in high school past age 18?

Does your child have the reading and math skills needed to live as independently as possible in the community? Are there financial considerations related to her leaving school or getting a job? For example, if your child is no longer a full-time student and not considered disabled enough to receive Medicaid, she could lose health insurance coverage when she leaves school (assuming your health insurance policy only covers dependents who are full-time students).

These recommendations uncover and address the obstacles to your child's dreams and goals early in the process. Then, you have an entire support system in the IEP team to help you and your child overcome each obstacle. It is also important to remember that even parents of students who do not have disabilities are going through some of the same things that you are. Their children may be initially focused on college, but then during senior year decide that they do not want to go. Perhaps a student has been attending a technical school during high school and during the job experience decides this isn't what she thought it would be. It's OK if plans for your child change too. Step back, take a breath, and reach out to others for support.

If your child has not achieved a diploma and is under age 21, you can continue to work with her transition team and devise a new transition plan. If she is approaching age 21, or is on track to get a diploma, the educational team is limited in the help they can offer post-graduation. However, they would still likely point you in a direction that can provide assistance. After all, they want your child to succeed just as much as you do.

Not only should IEP transition teams be prepared for changes in the

51

student but also for changes in the laws and systems. For example, if your child is moving toward postsecondary education and your school district requires students to pass high stakes tests in order to graduate, the team must be aware of such requirements. Under the NCLB Act, accountability requirements for districts and students are changing yearly. It is critical that IEP transition teams be prepared to revise programs so that students can meet the specified criteria. Revisions that team members should be prepared to make to your child's IEP include:

Revising goals and objectives, adding related services such as assistive technology or behavior supports if they are not already included, providing tutoring, pre-teaching skills that will be needed, or adding accommodations or modifications to the IEP.

Additionally, the team needs to pay attention to the postsecondary program your child has selected and make adjustments to your child's instructional program if entrance requirements change or the program ceases to be available.

Transition Portfolio Planning Tool for Students with Autism Spectrum Disorders

Demographics

Name: _____

Date of Birth: _____

Street Address: _____

City/State/Zip: _____

Telephone:_____

Email:_____

Support Network:_____

_____

_____

_____

Family Contacts/Roles: _____

_____

_____

_____

Agency/Medical/Financial/Legal:_____

_____

_____

_____

About the Authors: Carolyn T. Bruey, Psy.D., BCBA, has been supporting individuals with autism spectrum disorders, their families, and educational settings for over thirty years. She is currently the Supervisor of School Psychologists and ABA Consultants for the Lancaster-Lebanon Intermediate Unit 13 in Lancaster, Pennsylvania, as well as the onsite administrator for the IU 13's center-based educational program servicing students with significant behavioral challenges. Dr. Bruey is the author of *Demystifying Autism Spectrum Disorders: A Guide to Diagnosis for Parents and Professionals,* as well as chapters in various books focusing upon best practices when supporting children and adults with autism spectrum disorders.

Mary Beth Urban, M.Ed., has been working with children with disabilities and their families for twenty-one years. Her work as a special education teacher and special education consultant for secondary programs provided her with a variety of experiences related to developing transition services for students, including those with developmental disabilities and those on the Autism spectrum.

Chapter 5

Educating Students with Asperger's Syndrome

Chapter 5

Educating Students with Asperger's Syndrome
Temple Grandin, Ph.D.

I am becoming increasingly concerned that intellectually gifted children miss opportunities because of labels such as Asperger's Syndrome or with high functioning autism. Within the last year, several parents concerned me by what they had to say. One mother called me and was very upset that her six-year-old son had Asperger's Syndrome. She then went on to tell me that his IQ was 150. I replied that before people knew about Asperger's Syndrome, their child would have received a very positive label of intellectually gifted.

...sometimes, we can change people's behaviors and attitudes, and everyone is appreciated...

—Jed Baker, Ph.D.

I Am What I Think And Do

As a person with autism, I base my sense of being on what I think and do. I am what I think and do, not what I feel. I have emotions, but my emotions are more like those of a 10-year-old child or an animal. My life has meaning because I have an intellectually satisfying career that makes life worth living. In my work designing livestock facilities, I have improved the treatment of farm animals and I have been able to travel many to interesting places. I have traded emotional complexity for intellectual complexity. Emotions are something I have learned to control.

It is essential that talented children labeled either with high-functioning autism or Asperger's Syndrome be trained in fields such as computer programming, where they can do intellectually satisfying work. As for many people with Asperger's Syndrome, for me my life is my work. Life would not be worth living if I did not have intellectually satisfying work. I did not fully realize this until a flood destroyed our university library. I was attending the American Society of Animal Science meetings when the flood occurred. I first learned about it in a story on the front page of USA Today. I grieved for the "dead" books the same way most people grieve for a dead relative.

The destruction of books upset me because "thoughts died." Even though most of the books are still in other libraries, many people at the university will never read them. To me, Shakespeare lives if we keep performing his plays. He dies when we stop performing them. I am my work. If the livestock industry continues to use equipment I have designed, then my "thoughts live" and my life have meaning. If my efforts to improve the treatment of cattle and pigs make real improvements in the world, then life is meaningful.

I have been reading with great satisfaction the many articles in magazines about Linux free software. People in the business world are not able to comprehend why the computer people give their work away. I am unable to think about this without becoming emotional. It is no mystery to me why they download their intellectual ideas into a vast, evolving, and continually improving, computer operating system. It is because their thoughts will live forever as part of the "genetic code" of the computer operating system. They are putting themselves into the operating system—and their "intellectual DNA" will live forever in cyberspace. As the program evolves and changes, the code they wrote will probably remain hidden deep within it. It is almost like a living thing that is continually evolving and improving. For both me and for the programmers that contribute to Linux, we do it because it makes our lives more meaningful.

Continuum of Traits

There is a continuum of personality and intellectual traits from normal to abnormal. At what point does a brilliant computer programmer or engineer get labeled with Asperger's Syndrome? There is no black and white dividing line.

Simon Baron-Cohen, an autism researcher at the University of Cambridge, found that there were two times as many engineers in the family histories of people with autism. I certainly fit this pattern. My grandfather was an engineer who co-invented the automatic pilot for an airplane. I have second and third cousins who are engineers and mathematicians. At a recent lecture,

Dr. Baron-Cohen described three brilliant individuals with Asperger's Syndrome. There was a brilliant physics student, a computer scientist and a mathematics professor. It is also likely that Bill Gates has many Asperger's Syndrome traits. An article in Time Magazine compared me to Mr. Gates. For example, we both rock. I have seen videotapes of Bill Gates rocking on television. Articles in business magazines describe his incredible memory as a young child.

There is evidence that high functioning autism and Asperger's Syndrome have a strong genetic basis. G.R. DeLong and J.T. Dyer found that two thirds of families with a high functioning autistic child had either a first or second-degree relative with Asperger's Syndrome. In the *Journal of Autism and Developmental Disorders*, Sukhelev Naragan and his co-workers wrote that educational achievement of the parents of an autistic child with good language skills were often greater than those of similar parents with normal children. Dr. Robert Plomin at Pennsylvania State University states that autism is highly heritable.

In my book, *Thinking in Pictures*, I devote an entire chapter to the links of intellectual giftedness and creativity to abnormality. Einstein himself had many autistic traits. He did not learn to speak until he was three years of age and he had a lack of concern about his appearance. His uncut hair did not match men's hairstyles of his time. Additional insights into Einstein are in *Thinking in Pictures*.

Genius May be an Abnormality

It is likely that genius in any field is an abnormality. Children and adults who excel in one area, such as math, are often very poor in other areas. The abilities are very uneven. Einstein was a poor speller and did poorly in foreign languages. The brilliant physicist Richard Feynman did poorly in some subjects.

A review of the literature indicates that being truly outstanding in any field may be associated with some type of abnormality. Kay Redfield Jamison, from Johns Hopkins School of Medicine, has reviewed many studies that show the link between manic-depressive illness and creativity. N.C. Andreason, at the University of Iowa, found that 80% of creative writers had mood disorders sometime during their lives. A study of mathematical giftedness, conducted at Iowa State University by Camilla Persson, found that mathematical giftedness correlated with being nearsighted and having an increased incidence of allergies. I recently attended a lecture by Robert Fisher at Barrow Neurological Institute in Phoenix, Arizona. He stated that many great people had epilepsy, including Julius Caesar, Napoleon, Socrates, Pythagoras, Handel, Tchaikovsky and Alfred Nobel.

Types of Thinking

There appear to be two basic types of thinking in intellectually gifted people who have Asperger's Syndrome or high-performing autism. The highly social, verbal thinkers, who are in the educational system need to understand that the thought processes of these people are different. The two types are the visual thinkers like me, and like the music, math, and memory thinkers described in Thomas Sowell's book, *Late Talking Children*. I have interviewed several of these people, and their thoughts work in patterns in which there are no pictures. Sowell reports that in the family histories of late talking, music, math, and memory children, 74% of the families will have an engineer or a relative in a highly technical field such as physics, accounting, or mathematics. Most of these children also had a relative that played a musical instrument.

Every thought I have is represented by a picture. When I think about a dog, I see a series of pictures of specific dogs, such as my student's dog or the dog next door. There is no generalized verbal dog concept in my mind. I form my dog concept by looking for common features that all dogs have and no cats have. For example, all of the different breeds of dogs have the same kind of nose. My thought process goes from specific pictures to general concepts, whereas most people think from general to specific. I have no vague, abstract, language-based concepts in my head, only specific pictures. When I do design work, I can run three dimensional, full motion "video" images of the cattle handling equipment in my head. I can "test run" the equipment on the "virtual reality" computer that is in my imagination. Visual thinkers who are expert computer programmers have told me that they can see the entire program "tree," and then they write the code on each branch.

It is almost as if I have two consciences. Pictures are my real thoughts, and language acts as a narrator. I narrate from the "videos" and "slides" I see in my imagination. For example, my language narrator might say, "I can design that." I then see a video of the equipment I am designing in my imagination. When the correct answer pops into my head, it is a video of the successful piece of equipment working. At this point, my language narrator says, "I figured out how to do it." In my mind, there is no subconscious. Images are constantly passing through the computer screen of my imagination. I can see thought processes that others have covered up with language. I do not require language for either consciousness or for thinking.

When I learned drafting for doing my design work, it took time to train my visual mind to make the connection between the symbolic lines on a layout drawing and an actual building. To learn this I had to take the set of blueprints and walk around in the building, looking at the square concrete support columns, seeing how the little squares on the drawing related to the actual columns. After I had "programmed" my brain to read drawings, the ability to draw blueprints appeared almost by magic. It took time to get information in, but after I was "programmed," the skill appeared rather suddenly.

Researchers who have studied chess players state that the best chess players have to spend time inputting chess patterns into their brains. I can really relate to this. When I design equipment, I take bits of pictures and pieces of equipment I have seen in the past and reassemble them into new designs. It is like taking things out of the memory of a CAD computer drafting system, except I can reassemble the pieces into three-dimensional, moving videos. Constance Milbrath and Bryan Siegal at the University of California found that talented autistic artists assemble the whole from the parts. It is "bottom up thinking," instead of "top down thinking."

Teachers and Mentors

Children and teenagers with autism or Asperger's Syndrome need teachers who can help them develop their talents. I cannot emphasize enough the importance of developing a talent into an employable skill. Visual thinkers like me can become experts in fields such as computer graphics, drafting, computer programming, automotive repair, commercial art, industrial equipment design, or working with animals.

The music, math, and memory type children can excel in mathematics, accounting, engineering, physics, music, and other technical skills. Unless the

60

student's mathematical skills are truly brilliant, I would recommend taking courses in library science, accounting, engineering, or computers. Learning a technical skill will make the person highly employable. There are few jobs for mediocre mathematicians or physicists. Since social skills are weak, the person can make up for them by being so good at something that they will be attractive as employees. Teachers need to council individuals to go into fields where they can easily gain employment. Majoring in history is not a good choice because obtaining a job will be difficult. History could be the person's hobby instead of the main area of study in school.

Many high functioning autistic and Asperger's teenagers get bored with school and misbehave. They need mentors who can teach them a field that will be beneficial to their future. I had a wonderful high school science teacher who taught me to use the scientific research library. Computers are a great field because being weird, or a "computer geek," is okay. Most companies recognize a good programmer for his or her skills. I know several very successful autistic computer programmers. A bored high school student could enroll in programming or computer-aided drafting courses in a local community college.

To make up for social deficits, the autistic person needs to become so good at their work that his brilliance is recognized. People respect talent. They need mentors who are computer programmers, artists, draftsmen, etc., to teach them career skills. Many ask me, "How does one find mentors?" You never know where a mentor teacher may turn up. He may be standing in the checkout line in a supermarket. I found one of my first meat industry mentors when I met the wife of his insurance agent at a party. She struck up a conversation with me because she saw my hand-embroidered western shirt. I had spent hours embroidering a steer head on the shirt. Post a notice on the bulletin board at the local college in the computer science department. If you see a person wearing a computer company name badge, approach him and show him work that the person with autism has done.

Sell Your Work, Not Your Personality

Since people with autism and Asperger's Syndrome are inept socially, they have to sell their work instead of their personalities. I showed my portfolio of pictures and blueprints to prospective customers. I never went to the personnel office. I went straight to the engineers and asked to do design jobs.

Another approach is to put up a web page that showcases work in drawing or programming. Freelance work is great. It avoids many social problems. I can go in, design the project, and then get out before I get social problems. There have been several sad stories where an autistic draftsman or technician has been promoted to a management position and ended up being fired or quitting. Employers need to recognize the person's limitations. An excellent draftsman, commercial artist, technician or computer programmer may lose their career when promoted to management.

Reward these people with more pay or a new computer instead of management jobs.

People with autism and Asperger's Syndrome need concrete, well-defined goals at work. For example, the job is to design a better speech recognition program. When one project is finished, give them another project with a well-defined goal. If too many projects crowd them all at once, they will become confused. Let the person with autism or Asperger's Syndrome finish the first project before giving another. The projects can be difficult but they must have a well-defined goal.

Teaching Citizenship

Since people with autism and Asperger's Syndrome are emotionally immature, they must have basic morality reinforced when they are small children. When I was little, I was taught in a concrete way that hurting other people, stealing and lying were bad. At age 8, I stole a toy fire engine, and my mother made me give it back. She told me "How would you like it if someone stole one of your model airplanes?" She also told me that you do not hit other kids because I would not like it if they hit me. It was the Golden Rule: "Do unto others as you would want them to do unto you." Some Asperger's Syndrome children and adults have done some bad deeds because they didn't understand basic rules. I live a rule-based life and I have a rule system I still use today.

Anxiety Problems

For many people with autism and Asperger's Syndrome, anxiety and nervousness is a major problem. I discuss this in detail in my book, *Thinking in Pictures*. Anxiety problems worsen with age. My anxiety became unbearable in my early thirties. It was like a constant state of stage fright. At times, my nervous system was so aroused that I felt as if a lion was stalking me, but there was no lion. I have talked to several people with autism who quit good, high-paying jobs in graphic arts when anxiety and panic attacks made going to the office impossible.

Many people with autism or Asperger's Syndrome need medication to control their anxiety. I have been taking antidepressants for almost 20 years. My career would be in ruins if I didn't start taking antidepressants to control my anxiety. I know many autistic and Asperger's adults that are taking Prozac or one of the other Serotonin re-uptake inhibitors. People need to understand that medications such as Prozac can improve their lives.

The anxiety is due to biological problems in the nervous system. Recent brain research is showing that there is immature development in certain parts of the brains of people with autism. Autopsies of brains of people with autism show that there are biological abnormalities that occur when the fetus is developing. Antidepressant medication helps reduce anxiety caused by biological problems in the nervous system.

Parents...What to Do Next?

Take one or more of the following steps:

Attend one or more parent support groups: Parents can be a wonderful source of support and information. There are over 200 chapters of the Autism Society of America, over 70 chapters of FEAT, and other informal parent support groups. Consider joining at least one.

Contact your state's Developmental Disabilities program and apply for services. Be persistent. Contact your local school district and ask about school programs. See what they have to offer.

Find a local physician, attend local and/or national autism conferences, and find time for your other family members. Autism can be challenging.

Continue trying to learn all you can.

About the Author: Dr. Temple Grandin presently works as a Professor of Animal Science at Colorado State University. She speaks around the world on both autism and cattle handling. Dr. Tony Attwood, world renowned expert on ASD, says this about Temple:

"Temple is my hero. She has my vote for the person who has provided the greatest advance in our understanding of autism this century." HBO recently featured Dr. Grandin in a special television series on autism titled, "Temple Grandin". She inspired millions with her story and advancements despite having Asperger's, and holds a place in history as the most famous woman with autism.

Dr. Grandin is the best selling author of multiple books, including, *The Way I See It: A Personal Look At Autism and Asperger's*; *Thinking In Pictures: My Life With Autism*; *Unwritten Rules of Social Relationships* and *Animals Make Us Human*.

Chapter 6

Communications

Chapter 6

Communications

Katya Hill, Ph.D., CCC-SLP and John Halloran, M.S., CCC-SLP

Competence is Key

...the future of autism means creating a better Quality of Life

—Barry M. Prizant, Ph.D.

Communication is vital, and one of the most difficult challenges with autism. Whether your child is verbal or non-verbal, people with autism don't process information in the same way as the so-called, 'neurotypical' people do. Their communication style is more concrete than abstract. For example, if you say, "It's raining cats and dogs," your child might look up to the sky to see if cats and dogs were coming down. How about: "Let's toast the bride," "Keep your eyes peeled," and so on....

When you communicate with a person with autism, pay very close attention to every detail, including body language and sensory issues, which may affect language and comprehension.

Autism, Communication, and AAC

Katya Hill, Ph.D., CCC-SLP

One of the most exciting events in a parent's life is hearing their child speak his or her first word.

However, for parents of many children with autism, the early excitement of their child saying the first words and phrases is replaced by silence. For other parents, the first spoken words never happen. Yet, for other parents, their child may be repeating words, but not using words to communicate purposefully or take turns and show an interest in conversations.

66

Unfortunately, professionals cannot answer why this happens when parents ask the question, but we can provide suggestions to start showing gains in language and communication skills.

First, you'll want to understand the distinction between speech, language, and communication. Before you can understand what your younger or older child isn't doing, you need to know what they should be doing. Once you are empowered with the information regarding language-based interventions, you will be able to successfully make changes in your child's educational program.

Difference Between Speech, Language, and Communication

Speech involves the use of our respiration, voice and oral-motor movements to produce and say words.

Language is a system for encoding and decoding information; i.e., the ability to understand what is said to us and then put words together to form a message others understand.

Vocabulary and grammar are essential skills to use language effectively along with learning social rules and functions.

Communication is the process of exchanging information. Therefore, communication involves sending a message using our speech and language skills. This means that your tone of voice, the volume, vocabulary and sentence structure affect the meaning of our communication as well.

Most parents I work with who have children with autism, believe their child's behavior problems or "tantrums" stem from the fact that their child has no way of really telling them want they want, what's wrong, or what happened to make them upset. It's very important, then, to have ways for your child to communicate with you.

Parent Tip: With no words, the most effective way for your child to protest may be to scream, cry, push, run, and generally act out.

What is ACC?

Augmentative and Alternative Communication (AAC) is a term used to describe the various strategies and methods which address the expressive communication needs of people with significant speech disability.

AAC interventions can provide great benefits for your child at any age. AAC interventions range from using signs and gestures, picture symbols on cards and wallets to high-technology voice-output devices. Children with autism may use several AAC systems over a lifetime. When properly recommended and selected, AAC intervention is the opportunity for children with autism to show gains in speech, language, and communication abilities—and maximize their potential.

Before using AAC, it is important for parents and professionals to identify the major transitions in language development that typical children move through before entering school. Table 1 identifies and describes the three main transition periods in language development. Let's take a closer look at these transitions, so we can appreciate how AAC interventions have to be designed and introduced in order to build communication competencies with specific language skills taken into consideration.

We'll describe the three transitions as:

1. Early language—intentional communication and vocabulary learning –begins between 12 and 18 months

2. Building language—putting words together and making sentences;

3. Mastering language and literacy—learning to read and write.

This early transition period is short, and once children have about a 50-word vocabulary, they are probably into the second transition that includes learning many more words, along with word order and grammar.

Table 1. Major Transitions in Language Development for Typical Children

Typical age in development	Description of transition	Language functions	Transition terms used by professionals
12 months	Early language—intentional or purposeful communication and vocabulary learning. Children move from babbling a variety of sounds to saying their first words.	Social language functions transition from growing vocabulary skills to communicating to regulate a variety of social functions, e.g., requesting, greeting, taking turns.	Pragmatics → Semantics
18 months	Building language—putting words together and making sentences. Children move from saying single-word utterances to uttering simple multiword sentences. Simple sentences grow in complexity and variety.	Vocabulary continues to grow as grammar skills are needed to build communication competence.	Semantics → Syntax
4-6 years	Mastering language and literacy—learning to read and write. Listening and speaking skills grow and children learn about letters and sounds.	The basic sounds and grammar of a language have been acquired as skills are applied to reading and writing a language.	Phonology → Metaphonology

The second transition starts around 18 months of age and lasts until almost the start of school. This is the longest transition, because children add many words to their vocabulary, develop all the basic rules of grammar, and increase the complexity of their sentences.

As children move through the first two transitions, they are gaining skills that prepare them to read and write. They are holding and turning pages in books, properly looking from left to right. They are identifying logos and signs in the environment. They are speaking the repeating phrases in books and pretending to read to their parents. They are scribbling on paper pretending to write, and their writing improves in appearance to standard letters.

This third transition depends on many things; one of which is child having fluent expressive language (speaking) skills.

Once you know the developmental milestones related to language and literacy skill, you will see when and why it may be critical to investigate and implement AAC.

4. All children go through the same transitions in language development regardless of the disability or the delay. However, each child is an individual and will go through these stages at his or her own pace. That is why AAC uses interventions which duplicate or shadow the natural process of language and literacy development.

5. Language considerations, or how language is represented and generated using an AAC system, takes precedence over any instructional or technology innovation. Savvy parents and professionals realize decisions about AAC interventions are made based on the child's language first, and technology considerations second.

AAC Interventions for Children with Autism

The goal of AAC is to give children the means to say what they want to say, and it's important that parents understand what a child is thinking and feeling.

Parent Tip: Parents, you don't need to become experts on AAC strategies and technology. You are the experts on your children.

You do need to be involved in making decisions about how your child's language is represented via messages (sentences) constructed by your child. The three methods used with AAC interventions are:

1. Alphabet-based
2. Single-meaning picture symbols
3. Multiple-meaning picture symbols (Semantic Compaction Systems)

Once your child begins to use an AAC device, be sure to discuss the pre-programmed messages, because each child is unique. At first it may appear as if they don't like the device, when if fact, it has to be pre-programmed to their needs. It's important to discuss these things with your child's speech and language therapist.

That leads to the next language topic, which is insuring that your child has all the "core" words necessary to speak in sentences. Core words are not nouns, but the high frequency words needed to communicate. Examples are I, you, it, is, are, on, off, but, because, sure, go, to, etc. In your discussions about AAC, you'll be choosing the right words to work on to build communication, and help your child during childhood, and as he or she transitions to adulthood.

AAC interventions can fit into the three language transitions talked about earlier, and these interventions will not hinder your child or loved one's speech; they will only enhance their ability to communicate.

In addition, AAC interventions can also improve reading and writing skill development.

In summary, parents who keep in mind the notion that language is the critical component of AAC interventions, and not the bells and whistles of the latest technology. You want to start by supporting early language milestones in order for your child to say what he or she wants to say. Do not accept functional communication as the end goal, but advocate for language competence. Then you know your child is ready to learn and go about selecting activities that will create a shared focus with communication partners. Your efforts will move your child with autism from partner-dependent communication to a lifelong independent communicator.

Parent Tip: Be fully informed of all the options, and use a range of AAC interventions, depending on the situation.

Resource: I helped co-found the AAC Institute, a non-profit organization dedicated to the most effective communication possible for individuals who cannot speak. As an Internet-based organization, we provide resources and tools to support evidence-based decisions about AAC interventions. In addition, we advocate for consumer protections related to AAC services, funding practices and policies. One of the resources we are most proud of is the AAC Parents' Corner.

Go to the AAC Institute's Website at www.aacinstitute.org and visit the Parents' Corner. Robin Hurd, a parent with four children, three with disabilities, writes a monthly column and manages the AAC Parents Google Group, a discussion board for parents only. This is a safe place for parents to post questions, air their concerns, and get support from other parents who may be facing similar challenges. You can write to Robin at parents@aacinstitute.org. Since I'm a professional, I don't get to participate in this discussion forum. However, parents volunteering to help out the AAC Institute frequently share how this resource helps to keep them positive, face conflicts, and offers friendships they never thought they'd have.

If you're reading this book, you have already acquired knowledge and skills to do so. Yet, many of the policies and accepted practices of special education, funding regardless of the source, rehabilitation, assistive technology, and AAC services, do not seem as family-centered as intended. In fact, after reading this book, you may be more empowered and informed than some of the professionals or practitioners delivering services to your child. We encourage you to work with us as we try to maximize the potential of individuals with autism who need AAC, one child at a time.

Parent Tip: Do not let go of your dreams for your child.

About the author: Katya Hill, Ph.D., CCC-SLP is an internationally recognized speaker in the field of Augmentative and Alternative Communication (AAC). Her career reflects her mission of improving the quality of life for children with autism by advocating for the most effective communication possible. Dr. Hill is a speech and language pathologist with over thirty years of clinical and teaching experience. Currently, she is an Associate Professor in the Department of Communication Science and Disorders at the University of Pittsburgh where she conducts research on AAC performance measurement and language activity monitoring. Dr. Hill is a co-founder of the AAC Institute and ICAN Talk Clinics a worldwide resource for AAC education, clinical services and research. She is also the Executive Director of the AAC Institute.

Max Finds His Voice:
Language Acquisition Through Motor Planning
John Halloran, M.S., CCC-SLP

Current literature estimates that up to 60% of children diagnosed with autism will not have functional communication skills by high school. This is taking into consideration all the methods of teaching language and implementing Augmentative and Alternative Communication (AAC) currently held as best practices. While current methods meet the needs of some children and offer enrichment to all, too many children are not given the opportunities they deserve.

In this section, I'd like to offer you a therapeutic approach, called LAMP (Language Acquisition through Motor Planning) to teach non-verbal individuals to communicate through the use of a device with speech output. The device allows the individual to press keys to hear words spoken by the device.

Each word on the device is activated by a different key or series of keys so that the motor movement to say each word is unique.

When we talk, each word is formed by a unique series of movements with our mouth. When a motor movement to perform an activity remains constant, after some practice, we are able to perform those movements without thinking about them.

When we speak, we don't have to think about how to move our lips and tongue to form the words. This allows us to focus on the topic and flow of the conversation and allows us to communicate.

Having a unique motor pattern for each word on an AAC device makes it easy to use the device without having to look for certain pictures, understanding categories, or navigating through pages to find words.

The words available on the device include not only nouns for requesting, but other parts of speech which make up the majority of the words we use to communicate. LAMP takes your child's sensory needs into account as well.

Meet Max

Five-year-old Max was non-verbal. His parents were told that Max would probably never talk. He spent most of his time alone, watching videos or playing with his trucks, but not in a very purposeful way. He had no communicative sounds except for squealing to avoid an activity he didn't want to do or couldn't understand. To communicate, he relied on picture symbols to request items but usually had to be cued to initiate the request. "Show me what you want Max." He used about thirty signs he had learned according to his understanding of the sign. For example, when taught to nod his head "yes," an adult would place their hand on his head to help him nod.

Max understood this to be part of the sign, so his "yes" consisted of his hand on his head while he nodded. Eventually, he dropped the nod and just tapped the top of his head. While family members understood Max's signs, other people did not.

When it was time for Max to start school, his mother checked out his options. She observed regular kindergarten classrooms. She saw other five-year-olds sitting in their chairs, paying attention, learning to read, counting, and writing their names. Based on what she had been told, she thought Max would never be able to do those things. Max was enrolled in a self-contained classroom where he could receive individualized attention to meet his academic needs. After grade two, with little improvement, and increasing behavioral problems and outbursts, LAMP entered Max's life.

Max's educational team decided to explore the use of a speech-generating device implementing the LAMP therapeutic approach. During the initial consult, Max was able to learn and use several core words such as "go," "more," "up," and "stop" by pairing the unique motor pattern with the auditory output and a natural consequence.

In just a short six months, Max immediately used the handful of words he had been taught during his initial consultation. Over the next months, he used the device in class and therapy to learn more vocabulary. He played with the device on his own, learning as he explored. As he learned more words, he began putting them together into phrases and simple sentences.

In Max's case, an augmentative communication device and LAMP were the tools he needed to be able to express his current knowledge and build on it. He began "talking" about things that interested him. He liked going for drives and would label and talk about stores, streets, and objects around town. He particularly liked fences. He would point out a fence and his parents would use the opportunity to teach more vocabulary, like "brick fence," "big fence," "wood fence," and "white fence." Max began giving directions while in the car such as "turn left," "stop," "go Walmart," or "buy groceries." He could express his wants, comment on things he saw, and talk about things he liked.

This system allowed him to use language in the way that speaking people communicate–with words put together to express unlimited messages, and a unique motor pattern for each word paired with auditory output so that everyone could understand what he was "saying." Max's language skills grew by leaps and bounds.

Then Max began to sit, listen, and participate in classroom activities. He used his device to read along in class, and thrilled his teacher by independently completing reading comprehension worksheets. Max found words on his device so that he could use the text display to spell them.

That way, the device helped make his utterances easier to understand. Max literally transformed his house into a miniature model of his hometown, with cutouts of stores, signs, and streets correctly arranged and labeled.

Max became more interactive, initiated communication often, and was less frustrated. His mother said the greatest change was that "he went from watching things going on around him to being a participant." Last Christmas, he was able to do the opening announcement for the Christmas program at school and enjoyed doing it. The ability to communicate has opened many doors to opportunities and avenues that seemed unavailable to him before.

Today, at age ten, Max is primarily a verbal communicator. The quality of his speech is not perfect, but those who know him well usually understand him. He keeps his device close by in case the listener needs a little help.

Max's story is inspirational, because LAMP helps everyone understand that kids with autism have hidden skills and it's best not to get stuck on prerequisites before giving them a way to communicate. True communication encompasses so much more than requesting, and you'll want to look for options that don't limit your child's potential by a system or your own, or other's expectations.

About the Author: John Halloran is a speech and language pathologist, and Senior Clinical Associate for The Center for AAC and Autism. He received his Masters Degree in Communicative Disorders from the University of Arkansas for Medical Sciences in 1992. He has worked in the field of AAC since 1994 and has taught augmentative communication at local universities. He was the primary developer of Language Acquisition through Motor Planning and trains therapists, educators, and parents nationally on developing language and communication through AAC.

Chapter 7

Autism Through New Eyes™

Chapter 7
Autism Through New Eyes™

How to Improve Your Child's Reading, Writing, Coordination and Sports Abilities

Pat Wyman, M.A.

...if you keep doing things and getting exposed to things that help you... you get better...

—Dr. Temple Grandin

Would you like reading, writing, coordination and sports to be easier for your child? This chapter shows you how, along with several treatment options, which you can implement in an easy and very practical way.

As you think about your child's needs, today and in the future, eyesight, visual processing skills, visual perception, eye-hand coordination, visual-motor coordination and more, affect nearly everything your child does. This includes reading, writing, running, eating, speaking, picking up objects, watching television, using play equipment and everything in between.

Answer the following questions to help determine whether your child has undetected eyesight or vision problems, which if solved, will enhance your child's quality of life in a significant number of ways.

Did Your Child Experience Delays in Any of These Areas?

- crawling
- walking
- climbing stairs
- sensory abilities
- using playground equipment
- fine motor abilities, like writing with a pencil
- gross motor abilities like riding a bike

If you answered yes to some or all of these questions, although you may not see your child's stress in trying to avoid it, your child will very likely experience problems in reading, comprehension, writing, coordination, sports, language, driving, and much more.

Missing any motor milestone affects your child's ability to see properly and make meaning from, or interpret what they see. These delays affect what is known as visual processing and a whole host of other visual and motor tasks. What's more, research shows that nearly one half of people with autism, compared to 4% of people in the regular population, have an eye turn, or strabismus.

Imagine how these things affect your child. Have you ever looked at something through a distorted, clear object? See if you can find a drinking glass in your home, which has a lot of lines or other muti-dimentional decorations on it. Turn that glass at a 45 degree angle, look through the part where the most decorations are (usually near the side toward the bottom), and then try reading the words on this page. If you picked the right type of glass, you should see very distorted print, and have a bit of a clue as to how the world may look through your child's eyes.

Does Your Child Do Any of These Things?

- look sideways, through or around objects

- avoid looking you directly in the eye

- bump into things, squint to see, close or cover one eye

- show sensitivity to light

- act confused if you change the flooring in your home

- have difficulty climbing stairs or using playground equipment

- rub their eyes, hold or touch walls or tables when walking

If you answered yes to some or all of these questions, it means your child has a visual or a visual processing problem. When you read the information below, you'll discover how to treat this and make it easier for your child to read, write, play sports, be more at ease in social situations and make life better in countless other ways.

(Note: As with any treatment, you are the expert when it comes to your child. Depending on your child's unique needs, you may or may not want your child looking you directly in the eye, as this has different consequences for everyone. So, while these treatments can allow your child to do this, you will make the choice as to whether this is best for your child).

Many children and adults with autism don't see the world around them, or the words on a page the same way you do. If your child reads, you may notice that he skips lines, doesn't see punctuation, knows the word on one page and not the next, turns letters or words around, tells you the words jump off the page, or makes lots of other errors which affect comprehension.

Or, your child may be hyperlexic, able to read words at age two, just like Karen's son, Jonny. However, reading words and comprehending those words don't usually go hand in hand with hyperlexia.

Honestly, unless you know how the world looks through your child's eyes, (even though so many other things going on in your child's life) it can be easy to dismiss all these challenges, thinking it's due to the autism, and won't change.

But...

The Good News. You can start today and literally change your own world, and your child's for the better. I call this system, Autism Through New Eyes™. Here are the steps:

Read the Chart at the End of This Chapter

This chart shows which visual skills are required for reading and learning success. You can quickly see which skills a person needs, precisely for what purpose. This chart is reprinted with permission, from the Optometric Extension Program Foundation and The College of Optometrists in Vision Development.

Take Your Child to a Developmental Optometrist During Infancy. If Your Child is Older, Make This Visit a High Priority.

Eyesight is simply the ability to see something. Vision however, is the ability to make meaning from what you see. No matter how old your child, he or she needs a comprehensive eyesight exam, to check for eye health and determine how clearly things look at near and at far, plus a comprehensive vision exam, which will determine the underlying causes of and treatment for reading, writing, coordination, sports and many other challenges your child may have. You want to get these exams from an eye doctor who specializes in both.

These doctors are called developmental optometrists, behavioral optometrists or neuro-optometrists. They've had years of extra training to help children and adults improve visual skills which affect nearly every aspect of their lives. Gold medal winning athletes, Major League Baseball and National Basketball Association players often use a developmental optometrist's services in vision therapy, because it gives them what they call a "winning edge" of visual skills so they can be the best at what they do, and realize their full potential.

If you have an infant, a developmental optometrist can help you prevent a large number of eye health and visual processing problems, thus allowing your child to read, write, and have better coordination. This screening, early in life, can save you and your child years of anguish. Visit www.InfantSee.org and you will hear from former President, Jimmy Carter, why it is so critical to have your child's eyes examined as an infant.

If your child is older, you'll want to find out quickly, whether any of your child's reading or other challenges mentioned above, are visual in nature and what to do about it if they are.

You can find these doctors at: www.covd.org, www.oep.org and www.PaveVision.org.

Best selling author, Dr. Temple Grandin, the most well-known woman in the world with Asperger's, writes this in her book, *Thinking in Pictures: My Life with Autism:* "If visual processing problems are suspected, the child should see a developmental optometrist. This is a special eye doctor who can do therapy and exercises that help the processing problems that are inside the brain. In many of these children, the eye itself is normal but faulty wiring in the brain is causing the problems."

On a personal note, my daughter struggled with reading problems in the first grade, even though she could read at age 4. I took her to a developmental optometrist then, and she had vision therapy (a series of in-office sessions to correct visual and perceptual problems.) Today, she is a pediatrician and well on her way to becoming a Neonatologist. While my daughter was completely devoted to achieving her dream, I am certain it would have been much more difficult, if not impossible, had she continued to have the visual processing problems she had when she was young.

Once you get the comprehensive vision screening for your child, your child may need vision therapy. If your child needs vision therapy, check out the www.covd.org site for insurance information. Some parents get this funded through local Rotary and Lions' clubs, and other sources.

Once your child has vision therapy, your child's future will be brighter than you can ever imagine, in just about every possible way.

Know That School Vision Screenings are Incomplete and That 20/20; Eyesight Scores are Not Related to Reading at Near Point

On the way to raising reading and writing scores, it is crucial that you know school vision screenings are not comprehensive enough to diagnose the health of your child's eyes or determine whether the foundational skills for reading exist.

In chapter 16 of this book, Eric Chessen mentions that sports are branches and physical fitness is the roots and trunk. Incomplete vision screenings are the same. They are branches, which may be nearly disconnected to the tree trunk. When you don't examine a child's eyes to see if the skills needed to read, it's like building the roof before laying the foundation of your home.

The question I ask in my keynotes and seminars, is, "How many children or adults do you know who read a book, from 20 feet away, while covering one eye?"

Most schools use a single screening device and send you a score afterward. This is called the Snellen Eye Chart, which is for distance eyesight screening only. Most schools do not have the funding, personnel or equipment to perform the type of comprehensive eye exam your child needs.

20/20 eyesight simply means your child can see a letter, 3/8 inches high, from 20 feet away. This chart tells you nothing about what is happening when your child reads a book, copies from the book to a paper, or how your child feels when reading. It can never take the place of a developmental optometrist who can diagnose more subtle items such as visual perception, eye turns (strabismus), or lazy eye (amblyoplia), which, if left untreated, can lead to blindness.

Give Your Child an Auditory, Speech and Language Evaluation

Speech and language go hand in hand with good reading skills. It is essential that you rule out barriers that may be hampering your child's ability to read. Take your child to a certified speech and language pathologist, as well as an audiologist who is trained to evaluate both hearing, and how language sounds (auditory perception) to your child. Some speech and language pathologists are also audiologists, so ask before seeing two clinicians.

Where to Find Speech Language Pathologists and Audiologists

Visit www.asha.org, to find the best person for your child in the United States and Canada. This site has a full list of programs with audiologists, speech and language pathologists. Outside of the United States and Canada, do an Internet search for audiologists and speech and language pathologists in your area.

Make sure that the person you select is certified by the primary certifying organization for these professionals. If you don't know what that this association is, you can ask your local school for more information. You will want exams that include receptive and expressive language, as well as auditory perception, which is the ability to identify, interpret, and add meaning to sound. Also, look at Chapter 5 again, to discover more about Augmentative and Alternative Communication (AAC) interventions.

The demands on your child's visual system increase with each passing year, and again, you must know how the world looks through your child's eyes. If you suspect your child has an eyesight or vision problem, which may very well be undetected as you are reading this, the sooner you know, the sooner you can have it corrected, saving years of frustration for everyone.

Use Colored Overlays to
Help Your Child See the Printed Page More Clearly

Numerous research studies show that children and adults with ASD can benefit from using a colored overlay placed over the printed page.

A colored overlay is a piece of colored plastic, which is placed over a printed page, and research shows that various colors will clear up print, which often looks distorted without the overlay. Overlays can also reduce visual stress, and I've used them with children, parents, teachers, and even business executives for over 25 years, to help make reading faster and easier.

Most recently, Ludlow, A. K.; Wilkins, A. J.; Heaton, P., researched the use of colored overlays, and the results were published in Autism Spectrum Disorders, v2 n3 p498-515 Jul-Sep 2008.

Their study showed that a significant number of children with ASD increased their reading speed over those children in the controls when using a colored overlay. The article also shows that textual clarity and overall performance improved, for children with and without intellectual impairment, when using a colored overlay.

"Participants with ASD, both with and without concurrent intellectual impairment, showed significant gains in performance when using an overlay. The beneficial effects of color overlays and the implications of these results for current neuropsychological models of ASD are discussed..."

Other studies in journals such as "The Reading Teacher," show that reading and fluency improve when using a colored overlay.

Where to Find Colored Overlays

While there are many colored overlays available, I believe they need to be very sturdy, 8 ½ inches wide by 11 inches long, so they cover the entire page. There are overlays available in a smaller ruler size, but they will confuse your child because they only cover a small area of print, while the rest in is their peripheral vision.

Visit www.HowToLearn.com/filters.html to find a set of five overlays, (two blues, one yellow, one red and one green).

This set comes with a free Eye-Q Reading Inventory ™ (which you can also take online at www.HowToLearn.com/IReadISucceed.html) and this helps you determine the underlying causes of reading problems based on a symptom checklist. You will want to give this checklist to your developmental optometrist when you take your child for a comprehensive vision exam.

Over the years, I've had hundreds of people tell me that taping these overlays over the computer screen can ease visual stress immensely.

When I think of your child and their life with autism, and how much difference you can make by "clearing up the world they see, it reminds me of the words by the famous poet, Robert Frost. In his poem called 'The Road Less Traveled', he says "I took the road less traveled by, and it has made all the difference." Rather than choose an unknown future, take that road less traveled, and give your child the gift of better eyesight, along with better abilities to make meaning from what they see, better coordination, sports and recreational abilities, and it will make all the difference, today and tomorrow.

About the Author: Pat Wyman, M.A., is "America's Most Trusted Learning Expert." As a speaker, she inspires audiences with her keynotes, seminars and breakouts, because her unique props quickly put the attendee in the shoes of a person with autism. Within minutes, people truly understand how to help a person or loved on the spectrum.

Pat is an educational consultant and author who obtains corporate sponsorships for books. She is the CEO and founder of www.HowToLearn.com, best-selling author of *Learning vs. Testing: Strategies That Bridge the Gap Between Learning Styles and Test Taking Success; Instant Learning for Amazing Grades;* and co-author in the IPPY, Book Of The Year in the Medicine Category, *The Official Autism 101 Manual.*

She is also a university instructor at California State University, East Bay, a legislative expert, who testifies on school vision screening legislation, specializes in solving reading and learning challenges, and has worked with special needs children and adults, including those on the autism spectrum, for over 25 years. Pat is a highly sought after speaker and a regular media guest on radio and TV, as well as a quoted expert in such publications as Woman's World, Nick Jr. Family Magazine, and The Washington Post.

Vision and Reading Skills Chart

Reprinted with Permission from The Optometric Education Program Foundation and The College Of Optometrists In Vision Development.

Vision Skills Needed for Typical Reading, Classroom and Other Tasks

Classroom Tasks	Visual Acuity	Tracking	Eye Teaming –Sustaining Alignment at Near	Eye Teaming – Sustaining Alignment at Far	Focusing - Simultaneous Focusing At Near	Focusing - Simultaneous Focusing At Far	Focusing - Sustaining Focusing At Near	Focusing - Sustaining Focusing At Far
Reading	X	X	X		X		X	
Copying (CB to desk)	X	X		X	X	X		X
Copying (at desk)	X	X	X		X	X	X	
Writing	X	X	X		X	X	X	
Discussion	X	X	X	X	X	X	X	X
Demonstration	X	X	X	X	X	X	X	X
Movies, TV	X	X			X		X	X
P.E., Dancing	X	X	X	X	X	X	X	X
Art, Crafts	X	X	X	X	X	X	X	X
Play	X	X	X	X	X	X	X	X
Computers	X	X	X	X	X	X	X	X
Taking notes	X	X	X	X	X	X	X	X

Classroom Classroom Tasks	Eye Hand Coordination & Visual Motor Int.	Peripheral Vision	Directionality	Form Perception	Visual Memory	Visualization	Figure Ground	Visual Closure
Reading	X	X	X	X	X	X	X	X
Copying (CB to desk)	X	X	X	X	X	X	X	X
Copying (at desk)	X	X	X	X	X	X	X	X
Writing	X	X	X		X	X	X	X
Discussion		X	X	X	X	X	X	
Demonstration		X	X	X	X	X	X	
Movies, TV		X		X		X		
P.E., Dancing	X	X	X	X	X	X	X	
Art, Crafts	X	X	X	X	X	X	X	X
Play	X	X	X	X	X	X	X	X
Computers	X	X	X	X	X	X	X	X
Taking notes	X	X	X	X	X	X	X	X

Chapter 8

Tools for the Outside World

Chapter 8
Tools for the Outside World

Building Self-Esteem in Children with Autism and Asperger's Syndrome

...I am so glad that God has made this amazing person a part of my life

—Tiffany Sandlin

As the parent of a child with autism and a long-time autism expert, I can tell you without hesitation, that children and adults with autism have self-esteem problems. When you are critical of your child's behaviors or social interactions, they often feel hurt. They already feel as if they are under a microscope because of the doctor visits, occupational therapist sessions, testing, and stream of interventions we try. I'd feel like everybody was trying to fix me in the same set of circumstances and it would hurt my self-esteem too. I have enough problems feeling good about my cooking when my family criticizes me.

Kids with autism don't understand subtle jokes very often, and social interactions often turn out badly for them, which erodes their self-esteem even more.

Combine all this with the expectations of siblings and the all-too-frequent bullying, and it's easy to understand how devastated a child with an autism spectrum disorder can feel.

So, the big question I ask is, "What can we do?" It's crucial family members, educators, and professionals, learn strategies and techniques to build self-esteem in kids with autism/Asperger's. Everyone needs a reminder now and then, of just how precious they are, and our very special children need those reminders every day.

Parent Tip: Learn to correct behaviors by sandwiching the correction in the middle of positive feedback.

For example, "Sammy, you are doing a great job cleaning your room. If you pick up those clothes over there, it would look even neater. Boy, you sure are a good listener."

It Starts with Us

In order to build your child's self-esteem, you need to believe in your child's inherent value, and convey that to everyone else before self-esteem even begins to improve. These kids know when we're faking our compliments, and the therapy books say we should give five positive comments to each correction. We have to walk in our child's shoes and empathize with how they feel. We need to look for these special gifts, tune into the child with our hearts, and find ways to bring out their precious essence.

It helps when you go to conferences, read books, research and share information. Teach extended family, educators, and other professionals to help your child integrate into groups. Be intuitive when advocating for children, and persistent, not abrasive. In addition, keep a positive attitude.

Stay Positive and Emphasize The Positive

Children with autism oftentimes have an incredible sense of humor. I have to stop myself from laughing so my own son doesn't feel like I'm laughing "at" him, causing him to feel inadequate. Sometimes I'll even say, "I'm not laughing at you, Jonny, I'm laughing with you."

Emphasize the positives! Look for the good in every child, even if you don't see it at first. Model a mental attitude of "things are great." Express yourself in the positive, rather than the negative. Kids with autism/Asperger's are masters at copying what others say, so make sure they're hearing things that are good for them to copy! When we say, "you are great!" to a child often enough, he, too, will believe it and feel valued for who he truly is.

Encourage children to share their thoughts and feelings. This is so important and often sheds new light on existing situations.

Balance the Physical with the Mental and Spiritual

Like most people, kids with autism feel better about themselves when they're balanced physically, emotionally, and spiritually. These are all great ways to build self-esteem!

Since your child may have digestive problems, which often makes him or her a very fussy eater, likely to gravitate towards junk food, most doctors say it is important to try supplements. However, be sure and check with your child's doctor first. Also, provide regular physical activity, when possible, to relieve stress and clear your child's mind.

Set the stage for success by acknowledging their successes, however small, and reminding your child of their previous accomplishments. Keep their life manageable and don't overwhelm your child with too many activities.

Provide choices frequently so they understand they have a say in their own lives. You might want to try to give them a whole day when they are in charge of something. Give your child every opportunity to connect with their spiritual side, through religious avenues or by communing with nature. This can help them feel purposeful and that their lives have meaning.

One strategy that helped raise my Jonny's self-esteem, especially to overcome his victim thoughts and feelings, was spiritual affirmations. Using affirmations took some time, but we found that it brought calm and peace to Jonny and our family.

Dr. Jerry Jampolsky, the author of *Love is Letting Go of Fear,* and founder of the Center for Attitudinal Healing in California, offers many principles I find helpful in teaching us to love ourselves, thereby enhancing our own self-esteem and that of others. Some of his principles include:

The essence of our being is love; health is inner peace; live in the now; become love finders rather than fault finders; learn to love others and ourselves by forgiving rather than judging; choose to be peaceful inside regardless of what's going on outside; and we're all students and teachers to each other.

Part of Dr. Jampolsky's message is that by focusing on life as a whole, rather than in fragments, we can see what is truly important. His concepts, when embraced, positively affect how a child with autism thinks and feels about himself or herself. Anger, resentment, judgment, and similar feelings are all forms of fear. Since love and fear cannot co-exist, letting go of fear allows love to be the dominant feeling.

Look for the Miracles

Everyday, there are miracles and good things happening all around us. Be on your child's side by tuning into who they truly are: unique expressions of divine light. Empower your child to be O. K. with who they are. Do this by loving your child, not for who you want them to be, but for who they are. Consider that children and adults with autism/Asperger's are wonderful beings, here to teach us empathy, compassion, understanding, and most importantly, how to love. Do whatever it takes to authentically include your child in your life, rather than merely tolerate their presence.

As a gemologist, I learned that in genuine star sapphires, there are tiny imperfections and inclusions that reflect light perfectly, in order to form a star in the stone. Each child with autism is like this precious gem, unique in every way. Without the tiny inclusions, there would be no star. It is our job as parents, educators, and professionals to bring out the stars' in all of our special children by shining the light on their natural beauty. In doing so, we see their different abilities rather than their disabilities. In addition, then they will see them, too.

Social Stories
Bill Davis

Most of our children are visual learners. They gravitate towards videos and other visual learning tools. Children on the spectrum show very positive responses when presented with visual supports. When your child is young, you can rely on social stories to aid in the description of everyday events and to teach appropriate behaviors. The social story is an extraordinary visual tool that can be used to depict everyday activities such as playing with friends, bedtime, shopping, and interacting in a classroom setting. Social stories help our children learn what is expected of them in social situations. They can be individualized as well, to fit a person's routines and schedules.

Our children do not like surprises, and social stories illustrate the expected behavior and outcome. Our kids can then respond accordingly. Social stories are a straightforward tool for teaching social skills. They are detailed and specific. They focus on what the individual might expect and what reactions might be expected of him. Social stories have the ability to make the child more comfortable in different social situations.

Social stories are very structured and help address social impairments. They allow for a comfortable distance between teaching and actually being in the situation itself. There are three categories of social impairment:

- Social avoidance is when children try to escape from social situations. They may be overwhelmed by the environment or hypersensitive to sensory stimuli. Use the social story to address their needs.

- Social indifference is when kids do not seek interaction, but do not run from it either.

- Social awkwardness is usually found in higher-functioning children. When involved with a group of friends, they might not join in the conversation, but simply focus on their favorite subject or topic. Understanding social taboos is difficult for the person with Asperger's or autism.

Carol Gray developed social stories. They are not scripts. She believes that the child's personal need should be the motivation for the story. Your child's ability level is the basis for the story, and you will use the words "can" and "could" instead of "must" or "will." The learning process is greatly enhanced when paired with role-play.

As the child becomes proficient, phase in or faze out the stories, but hold on to them to use for review.

Carol Gray says, "A social story describes a situation, skill or concept in terms of relevant social cues, perspectives, and common responses in a specifically defined style and format."

Parent Tip: Write the social story from the child's perspective. Try and motivate behaviors and then demonstrate or show the expected response.

Karen's Story: One of the best, most effective tools I have used is a social story or a social story script. It's like writing an instruction manual of what you want to happen for your child.

94

One time I was having a difficult time convincing Jonny to get aboard an airplane to visit his grandparents. He was deathly afraid to fly, or so I thought. I even discussed medicating him with my doctor, just to get him on the plane. When I discussed the problem with his teacher's aide, she recommended that I write a social story script. We constructed a story that I typed out for Jonny that went something like this:

Jonny's Trip to Grani and Grandbunny's

- Mom and I drive to the airport in the car.
- We park the car and take our suitcases inside.
- We get a ticket at the ticket counter and give them our bags.
- We walk down a long hallway to where the plane is.
- Mom and I walk to get on the plane.
- We buckle our seatbelts and the plane goes up in the air.
- Everything looks small on the ground below.
- We fly for a while and read books.
- The plane lands and we get off to meet Grani and Grandbunny.
- Jonny looked at the paper, quickly read it, and threw it on the ground saying, "What if the plane blows up, and I have to parachute down."
- I immediately took the script and edited it, adding in two lines as follows and handed it back to him.
- Mom and I drive to the airport in the car.
- We park the car and take our suitcases inside.
- We get a ticket at the ticket counter and give them our bags.
- We walk down a long hallway to where the plane is.
- We go through a security gate to scan for concealed weapons.
- No one with anything dangerous is allowed on the plane.
- Mom and I walk to get on the plane.
- We buckle our seatbelts and the plane goes up in the air.
- Everything looks small on the ground below.
- We fly for a while and read books.
- The plane lands and we get off to meet Grani and Grandbunny.

After he read this he said, "Oh, okay" and he got on the plane with no problem at all! As your child transitions into adulthood, you can make these stories more age appropriate, and include things like employment and even college.

Using Pictures to Communicate, Storyboards and Video

- Storyboards are large boards with a series of arranged sketches in sequence. They outline the action of a film, story, or video. Storyboards may use captions. They will describe daily or future activities. Most are hand drawn. They can also point out the potential impact of an event. They are simply a sequential series of illustrations. Social stories can help motivate, define specific steps, or illustrate the student's goals.

- Video modeling is an effective method of teaching daily living skills. It seems to aid in generalization. It is a great tool for teaching conversation. Video modeling uses the child's propensity for visual learning by presenting a visual of the skill to be learned. Watching videos as a learning experience is highly preferred by children on the spectrum. It allows people with autism to view and examine a social situation as it is happening. Video modeling is an effective way for teaching social skills and helps in generalizing newly acquired skills.

Explaining Autism to Others

Autism can seem like a life sentence one moment and a spiritual celebration of life the next. At this point in time, autism is the fastest growing developmental disability. We constantly explain our children to people who don't want to understand. We define autism continually to educators who oppose us. We speak out because many of our children do not have a voice. Unity and fellowship seem to elude our movement. Some of us search for treatment, some for a cure, and some ask simply for adequate programming. Nonetheless, it should be all about the children.

According to an article by the American Academy of Neurology and the Child Neurology Society, "Autism and pervasive developmental disorders encompass a wide continuum of associated cognitive and neurobehavioral disorders, including the core defining features of impaired socialization, impaired verbal and nonverbal communication and restricted and repetitive patterns of behavior…"

There are several hundred different treatments offered for autism, with many viewpoints and a wide variety of theories.

So, how, with all this information around you, can you explain the sense of loss you feel when your child stops being who he was? It is like he's there, but he's not there. He disconnected.

How do you explain the sensory issues, the outbursts, and the pain your child wrestles with every day? How do you explain that autism is unique and unpredictable, but not horrifying? How do you explain the undying love and dedication we have for our children?

Look into your child's face, watch him smile, and you'll understand. No explanation is necessary.

The co-founder of Autism Speaks, Suzanne Wright, is adept at telling the world about autism. She spoke in Doha, Qatar at the Shafallah Center for Children with Special Needs. Her Highness Sheika Mozah Nasser al-Misaad, and Autism Speaks, are beginning discussions to collaborate and create a worldwide program for children with autism. The people at Autism Speaks have taken a huge step towards unity and understanding.

> **Parent Tip:** Parents need to advocate for their child because people just don't understand autism. They see our children as spoiled, undisciplined, mentally ill, or on drugs.

Explain, explain, explain autism to everyone, and then explain some more. Don't apologize for autism; shout it from the highest rooftop. Hold your head up high with all the confidence in the world, and let people know what is great about it and what is challenging. Help them to overcome their fear; the same fear you may have had before your child was diagnosed. They WILL understand, accept, and embrace your children especially if they understand them. If they don't, they are not worth knowing anyway!

Chapter 9

Safety Issues for Your Child

Chapter 9

Safety Issues for Your Child

Bill Davis

Law

Editor's note: No part of the information in this chapter is to be construed as legal advice, and if your child is in need of legal advice, contact an attorney.

Systems change has to begin with us

—Jan Randall

In order to protect our children, we must educate lawyers, judges, and juries about the behavioral issues associated with autism. People involved with the legal and penal system need to know that "outbursts" are due to pain, frustration, lack of communication, or sensory overload. We know that most inappropriate social interactions arise from misinterpreting social cues, facial expressions, the 'unwritten codes' of behavior, language, and commands.

Many studies show that people with disabilities have more contact with the criminal justice system than 'typical people.' If you have a child with autism who needs legal help, be sure an consult an attorney. They often recommend you employ the services of an expert witness to explain to a jury that the activity your child may have been involved in, is typical of, or caused by his autism. If an individual with autism is arrested, or involved in a criminal trial, then his autism has to be taken into consideration.

Lawyers say that a person cannot be found guilty solely because of autism. Autism alone, can never be the cause for conviction or suspension from school. If unfortunately, one of our children is found guilty of a crime, we hope the court will recognize his autism when considering sentencing or punishment. Incarceration can be horrific for a person with autism. They can easily be victimized in jail. Hopefully, any judge would opt for a residential treatment center in lieu of prison.

Parent Tip: Talk to your children about crime and illegal activities. Use social stories to distinguish between acceptable and harmful behaviors.

School and Community Law

I encourage you to review you and your child's rights in the Individuals with Disabilities Education Act (IDEA). Your child, under law, is entitled to a free and appropriate public education. Get involved and ensure an Individualized Education Program (IEP) and any special interventions your child needs to access that free and appropriate education are in place.

The Americans with Disabilities Act (ADA) is hugely important. People may not discriminate against your child because of the disability. Autism cannot be the cause or reason for refusal for housing, work or lodging. According to Autism Speaks, the Combating Autism Act of 2006 assigns approximately $108.5 million for NIH (National Institutes of Health) funded autism research. Including the other appropriations, about $162 million dollars are allocated for autism issues.

As parents and autism advocates, it is our job to make sure that our community and those who serve it (police, first responders, hospitals, firefighters) learn to identify a person with autism and have special knowledge of how to most effectively deal with them. We need to make sure our child with autism isn't treated the same as a typical person who is doing something wrong.

The people who help with, or take care of our children, need to know how to recognize a person with autism, how to approach, understand the behavioral issues, and ways to make the situation less traumatic.

The following are tips that you can share with your local police and firefighters as you work to make your community safer for your child:

Police

The police and other emergency service responders will encounter our children regularly. They may respond to medical emergencies or reported seizure activity. The police may intervene when behavior escalates or when the public, confused when observing an outburst, or a caregiver attempting to de-escalate his child's acting out, reports the incident to the local precinct.

We can always use more funding for first responder training, but you can also deliver a presentation in your own area. Contact the person in charge of training. Use outlines from this chapter or from my book, *Dangerous Encounters: Avoiding Perilous Situations with Autism*. Describe your child and his behaviors so your audience can put a face to the disorder. Leave your name and number as a resource and contact person. You don't have to pay a speaker to present when you are just as familiar with the subject yourself.

Parent Tip: Advocate, educate, and empower.

Autism Speaks advocacy organization is doing a wonderful job providing training for police, and generously shares their safety and training knowledge. They consulted with the Chicago Police Department and created a training video. Autism Speaks is enthusiastic about interacting with law enforcement, and are helping the police gain insight into the behaviors of people with autism.

Tips for the Police

When dealing with people with autism, keep in mind that you must try to be gentle, kind, quiet, and speak simply. Be aware that this person may:

- Find it hard to express his needs.

- Appear not be focused.

- Gesture with arms or hands to indicate needs.

- Offer no response.

- Be easily led into committing criminal acts.

- "Wander" and seek bodies of water (especially children).

- Be non-verbal or possess limited speech

- Repeat things over and over

- Repeat back what you say (echolalia)

- Use other forms of communication such as computers, icons, or sign. It is great if police carry "Silent No More" communication cards.

- Exhibit "flight-or-fight" behaviors.

- May not be aware of extreme temperatures.

- Exhibit seizures

- Avoid eye contact and sometimes do not understand or exhibit traditional body posturing. (Police react to body language, and focus on eye contact and gestures).

- Begin self-stimulatory behaviors like flapping or wringing hands.

- Play with spit and may bite.

- Touch their private parts, or the responder's.

- Have sensitivity to light, smells, textures, temperatures, and noise. Most kids love the K9 police dogs, but many of our children are frightened of animals because of their quick, unexpected movements.

- Obsessively refer to a topic that comforts them, like naming all the state capitols or different train models they have collected.

- Tips on approaching a person with autism:

- Look for personal ID, autism card, or handout.

- Remember our kids are visual; you might have to model desired behavior, show pictures or provide a written description.

- Use direct phrases.

- Understand that his response may be delayed.

- Be aware of your phraseology. Don't use idioms or abstracts, like "Cut it out!" or "Spread eagle!"

- Evaluate carefully for injury. People with autism can defer pain.

- Don't point or move suddenly.

- Do not try to stop his repetitive behaviors unless they are self-injurious.

- If you must arrest the person, try to keep him out of lockup. Allow for safe and tranquil surroundings.

- If you must use handcuffs, turn the person on his side. The autistic population traditionally has a weak upper torso region and may find it very hard to breathe when lying on their stomach. If they are vomiting or choking, they may not be able to indicate their distress to the police officer.

- Stay close, be intuitive, and keep the person calm.

About three years ago, I knew of a man in his thirties with autism, who died in a group home. He bit and became aggressive with his aide. The police used a stun gun, pepper spray, and then pinned him to the floor, facedown. We don't want this to happen any of our children, and is the reason we need to educate and advocate.

Working with Law Enforcement

Understanding autism is such a big learning curve for us, but as parents, we must all also learn to help professionals understand our children and autism.

Karen's Story: Recently my son, Alex who has ADHD, and I were invited to participate in a new program put on by the Los Angeles Police Department (LAPD). The purpose of the program was to educate the officers on how to handle the many delicate situations that can occur when involving the special needs population. They put forth several previously designed scenarios in which parents, along with their children, would act out different roles that would involve an officer.

My assigned scenario was to play the part of a homeless woman, with my son playing the part of a child with ADHD living on the street. My role was to convince Alex to steal some groceries from a convenience store. When caught, I had to resist my arrest and explain both my son's disability and my needs to the officers.

We all learned a great deal from this experience, as well as how little is known about proper handling of special needs individuals. I also gained tremendous insight into the police department, how they have to make instantaneous decisions regarding life, property, and the law.

Sometimes when a child with autism repeats back to the officer what he was saying, the officer likely will think the boy is making fun of him. What the officer doesn't understand is that people with autism often have "echolalia," which means they repeat back. Since kids with autism don't necessarily look different from their peers, lay people and law enforcement misinterpret their actions and think they should act and behave like so-called "normal" children.

There's still a lot to do, helping law enforcement professionals recognize and understand autism.

Firefighters and Rescue

Just think about how scary a firefighter looks with his mask on, the sound he makes as he breathes, how he moves through a building with a flashlight, splashing scary light around the room. The noises that fire makes, the sirens outside, the fear of the unknown, and the sights and sounds, all bring your child to an point of extreme confusion and anxiety.

What must you do to help your child make decisions in this situation, and how can we educate firefighters on helping your child survive, not just the fire, but also the rescue?

In Trenton, New Jersey, the Assembly Health and Senior Services Committee, released legislation to establish an Autism Awareness training course for EMTs, police, and firefighters. The new law, passed in March 2009, requires a course that educates responders in autism recognition and response. This measure (A-1908) is the final piece of the autism package, championed by Speaker Joseph J. Roberts Jr. It will aid in the detection, treatment, and awareness of autism. Bravo! However, as parents we must take action on our own as well, and work with politicians to pass similar laws in every state.

Tips for Parents

- Initiate an evacuation plan in case of fire. Frequently review the course of action.

- Utilize a safety social story. I illustrated fire safety stories in *Dangerous Encounters: Avoiding Perilous Situations with Autism.*

- Teach your child to respond when his name is called.

- Place a safety sticker on the child's bedroom window. This will alert firefighters that a child with autism lives in the home. Unlocking Autism has my safety sticker on their website, and the Autism Society of America has an excellent sticker as well.

- Provide information to your 911 center. Inform the fire department if your child is afraid of sirens, is non-verbal, suffers from seizures, and has an aversion to flashing lights. Tell 911 where he will retreat to in the house or elsewhere if they are looking for him.

- Make sure your street address is clearly marked.

- Introduce your children to the firehouse, the fire truck, and the firefighters.

Tips for Firefighters

- People with autism may unexpectedly move farther away when you attempt a rescue.

- Fire alarms and sirens might panic our children.

- They may suffer from seizure activity or sensory overload.

- Be calm when approaching a child with autism.

- Know that autistic children can defer pain to extreme heat or injury.

- Do not shout commands. Remain calm.

- Use short, simple, and repetitive requests.

- The child may retreat quickly. Please don't risk this occurring. It may come down to a very quick "grab and rescue."

- After rescue, it may be necessary to bring the child to a quiet place. The fire truck may be very frightening and overwhelming.

- Please check very carefully for injuries or burns. The person with autism may lack the ability to communicate their pain and fear. You may have to point to different body parts in order to ascertain if the child is injured.

- You may arrive for a medical emergency and a child with autism lives in the home. He may become very agitated. Please do not misunderstand his actions.

- Once again, be kind and patient. Contact the family or caregiver as soon as possible.

Personal Safety

Let's begin with safety in the home. Many of our children are "runners." They will bolt from school, the house or from play areas. If your child is a runner, please include this fact in the information that you provide the police and the 911 center. People with autism seem strangely attracted to bodies of water. Remember that it may be difficult for the person with autism to generalize. You may feel satisfied that you have taught your child pool safety, but he might not be able to carry what he learned to the lake or stream. A runner is also in danger of being exposed to criminal activity, predators, and a general population that will not understand his behavior or outbursts. Also, the child may not be dressed for the weather or be able to ask for food or help.

Tips on Home Security

- Have locks on all your doors and windows. You can find a good line of safety products at www.mypreciouskid.com.

- You may have to install Plexiglas windows if your child hammers away at them with his fists.

- Lock your cabinets and secure poisons and laundry products.

- Don't have too many shelves or bookcases around the home. Our kids can climb to the ceiling, using bedroom chest of drawers.

- In a way, you have to "baby proof" your house, like covering the outlets, hiding the knives, etc.

- Contact your local Poison Control Center and let them know about your child's habits, allergies, and seizures.

- You may want to install a security system in your home

- Use visual labels to aid in safety around the house, like "hot "and "cold," "STOP" signs, and that little "caution" symbol with the red circle and line drawn through it. This will help keep your child safe.

Parent Tip: Please give your child a voice! Signing, PECs, icons, and communication devices are all acceptable and necessary methods. He must have the ability to communicate.

Tips on keeping your child with autism safe

- This may sound odd, but always include your child in daily activities like washing the dishes and making the beds. Taking him shopping acclimates him and introduces him to society. This type of inclusion keeps him safer.

- Create an autism ID card or tag. Your child can wear a bracelet, a shoe tag or carry a card in his wallet. An alert card should contain the following:

  - personal contact information (name, address, phone number, etc.), characteristics (non-verbal, runner, biter, seizures or self-injurious)

  - an advocate's name and number

  - allergies, medications, etc.

  - include all this information in your own wallet about your child too

- Teach your child about personal space. Show him what standing "too close" is.

- Practice "good touch, bad touch," using a picture or a doll. Be clear on who is allowed to touch him, dry him off, dress, or bathe him. Teach your child to say "NO!" if touched or to put his hand out to indicate, "STOP!"

- Practice crossing the street. Inform his aides or caregivers to hold onto him. Let your child's caregiver know that he might bolt if he spies a dog, and to always hold his hand.

- Once again, please educate and alert your neighbors. If your child does "escape," get them involved before the police come. Also, show your child around the neighborhood. Have him become very familiar with his surroundings. Point out what doors he can knock on if he needs help.

Personal Safety Tips for the Person with Autism

- If you find yourself involved with the police, try to calm yourself. You may want to tell them that you have autism or mention just some relevant parts of your autism, for example, "I get nervous in situations like this," or "I find it hard to make eye contact."

- If you carry an autism ID card you might want to present it to the police. Do not put your hands in your pocket without asking permission first.

- Crime victims, ask the police to call your family.

- Make sure that you have the ability to describe any abusive situations. Bullying, pain, or past incidents of abuse must be communicated.

- Know your surroundings.

- Don't be ashamed to disclose your autism. Don't be a victim. Empower yourself.

Chapter 10

Out in the Community

Chapter 10

Out in the Community

Bill Davis

Shopping and Behavior in Stores

...tomorrow is a golden period for improvement and independence

—Tony Attwood Ph.D.

Meet with store owners ahead of time, and help them give you an improved shopping experience by educating them a bit about autism. Assure security and store owners that your child's odd behaviors are not crime or drug-related. Tell them that if they line things up, tear book pages or wander out of the store with unpaid merchandise, it is uncontrollable, and they don't mean to do anything wrong. We need to educate the public and legal system, to avoid police confrontations and foster a thriving society.

Keeping Your Child Safe While Traveling

Family vacations can be anything but typical, whether traveling with your younger or adult child. Kids tend to wander away, want to get on and off boats and other rides, and in and out of cars frequently. Let key people around you know more about your child, which will set a smoother course for the whole vacation.

Hotels

Use visual social stories prior to your trip, to illustrate what activities you will be doing. Use a calendar to demonstrate your travel plans. Alert hotel staff that you have a child with autism. Request an in-room fridge (for meds and special foods). Ask for a late checkout time. Make your child feel safe and secure. Double-check your packing list for comfortable clothes, favorite toys, "sensory" items, medications, DVD player and headphones, etc. Familiarize your child with his "boundaries" in the hotel room. Check windows, small spaces, outlets, and coffee pots for safety. Set up and rehearse a meeting place with the family and hotel staff, in case you and your child separate. Always teach your child to carry ID and know your room number. Parents, if you take turns, sharing the responsibility, and go on some outings by yourself, it can help ease the stress of traveling with a child with autism. Try to get wristbands for amusement parks and urge your child to stay close to you. People with autism may "bolt", resist procedures, bite, and become self-injurious at the sound of sirens and loud noises.

First Responders, Hospitals, and Emergency Rooms

The hospital experience can be quite taxing for a family that has a child with autism. The medical staff is overworked, parents are overwhelmed, and our children are on "overload." Tell the hospital staff how important it is to speed up the waiting time, and try to upgrade their place in the waiting list. Most children with autism will not have the patience to wait. Ask them to dim the lights and remove frightening medical devices in the exam room. Ease the child's anxiety with simple stories.

For Nurses, Doctors and Medical Caregivers

- Talk calmly, quietly and directly. Repeat your requests and allow time for response. Demonstrate procedures using pictures or signs. If the child is alone, look for handouts, ID's, or medical wristbands. Many people with autism have seizures, express pain by laughing, or have severe sensory issues. Avoid sudden or "light" touch. Watch for self-injurious behavior and look for injuries. Do not curtail repetitive behaviors or fixating on objects.

- Light, noise, touch, smells, or the feel of unfamiliar blankets may severely agitate your patient. They may understand more than you think and may be able to communicate in writing, pointing, signing, communication devices, or cards.

- Deep pressure while lying on their side can often calm your patient. Avoid sirens, flashing lights or sudden abrupt noises whenever possible. Waiting in the emergency room is extremely difficult for a child with autism.

113

- Keep talking, move slowly, and carefully explain where you are going to touch them with each step. Ask what comforts them and do not talk about frightening procedures. Understanding and sensitivity will make for a successful and safe encounter.

Parent Tip: If you are not satisfied with the treatment you and your child receive, request to speak with the head nurse. If necessary, ask to meet with the hospital administrator. That's advocacy!

Riding the Bus

Talk with school bus drivers well in advance of your child getting on the bus and show them how to facilitate communication cards and be adept at handling a child with autism during an emergency, fire, or accident. Parents can insist on audio-visual monitoring of the bus. Practice the bus route with your child before the beginning of the school year.

- Drivers should know how to stop self-injurious behavior and dealing with a non-verbal child who might need to use the bathroom during a long trip. They should also keep in mind a child may not know their bus number or bus stop.

- A note to bus drivers: keep the child in range of vision and maintain a behavioral management plan. Be aware of behavioral influences, such as route-changes, screaming, teasing or harsh lights. Know how to deal with seizures. Child seat belts are always necessary.

Public Restroom Use: Re-teach, Rethink, and Practice

Public restrooms are filthy, and loaded with germs and bacteria. Children with autism have immature immune systems and require special care. The public restroom can be over stimulating and potentially dangerous.

Teach the unspoken rules of privacy to your child. Here are some do's and don'ts for boys and girls. Don't linger, talk to, or make eye contact with strangers. Get your business done and get out of the bathroom. Lock the stall door before pulling pants up or down. Wipe off the seat first, put paper on it, and flush the toilet when finished. Put the toilet seat back down. Boys, if you use the urinal, pull pants down "just enough" and stand close to the urinal. Try to use a urinal that is not next to someone. If there are none, do not talk to the person at the urinal next to you. Do not play with the water in the sink or toilet. Wash your hands with soap and warm water and dry them. Girls: Do not flush sanitary napkins or other things that are not part of your normal "business" down the toilet. Wrap menstrual pads in tissue and put them in the appropriate disposal container, being careful not to touch any bits of paper in or around the disposal container.

When Getting a Haircut Is Torture

Sometimes we forget to consider our child's sensory issues with tasks like a haircut. You might want to ask a friend or family member to help and do this at home. It helps to explain this procedure to your child beforehand, using videos, social stories or scripts.

Post 9/11 Security, and Dealing with Extra Security

Security is tighter than ever so, carry cards or handouts that explain autism, in case you encounter special officers. Protect your child from misunderstandings by providing him with detailed ID. Remain with your child at all times, even during questioning. An interrogation could terribly upset a child with autism. Illustrate what is going to occur. Use social stories or illustrate what is going to occur and how to react. Alert authorities how overwhelmed your child may become around strange noise, alarms, flashing lights or waiting in line.

Our kids are very sensitive so don't leave the TV on all day when tragedies strike and dominate the news. We don't want our children to witness death and destruction, repeatedly. If they question the occurrences, answer them honestly but simply. Be direct and age appropriate. Try not to allow them to dwell on the subject.

Airports

If you feel any stress when traveling, imagine how your child might feel. Notify the airlines how certain stimuli can affect your child's behavior. Assure your child's safety and comfort by anticipating a "bumpy ride." Prepare your child with a social story, using pictures of the airport and airplane. Write numbered events for your child so they know what will happen, from beginning to end. Carry noise reducing headphones, and book non-stop flights if possible. Learn airline restrictions for fluids and other items you can bring in your carry-ons. If your child takes medications, be sure to check with the airlines ahead of time which you're allowed to bring, especially if they are liquid. If your child is on anti-anxiety medicine, check with the doctor about the best time to administer them. Busy airports and security check is stressful enough. Arrive early to eliminate extra stress and rush. Have your ID ready and ask to board early.

Chapter 11

Bullying

Chapter 11

Bullying

Bill Davis

Bullying is violence and abuse, and occurs with an imbalance in power. The victim may be intimidated, threatened, or physically attacked. Although we try to monitor our kids on the spectrum, bullying may take place when we are not present, without our knowledge, and worse, your child may not even realize he or she is a victim of this horrific injustice.

Autism tomorrow... is a dream of people accepting differences...

—Leighanne Spitzer

One day, I was sitting by a pool, and watched four teenage boys tease, splash, and ask a young man with Asperger's to swear. The boys were laughing at him, which delighted the man because he did not know he was being bullied. Fortunately, his father stepped in to stop them.

Bullying hurt my own son's self-esteem. Bullying can lead to long-term behavioral, emotional problems and even suicide. Watch for sudden behavior changes, depression, or withdrawal as possible symptoms of bullying and take your child for therapy immediately.

The Parents Role in Changing the Climate of Schools

It's painful enough to imagine bullies who hurt your child at school, but have you thought about teachers? "Teacher bullying gets little attention," says Stuart Twemlow, M.D., a psychiatrist who directs the Peaceful Schools and Communities Project at the Menninger Clinic in Houston. He says, "Teacher bullying uses power to punish, manipulate, or disparage a student beyond a reasonable disciplinary procedure."

Twemlow's new study, published in *The International Journal of Social Psychiatry*, hints that teacher bullying may be more common than people believe.

An anonymous survey from elementary school teachers showed that more than 70% believed bullying was isolated. However, a shocking, 45% admitted to bullying a student, or stood by, when students bullied each other!

If you want a Zero Tolerance policy for bullying in your school, you must respond instantly, when you see bullying.

Advocate, insist, and persevere if you want to change faculty, administrative, and support staff attitudes. Educate teachers about sensory issues for kids on the spectrum, so our kids feel they belong and successfully integrate into the system. Do not allow kids with autism to be separated or segregated in the school or community.

Here are some things you can do if bullying is a problem at school:

Form a committee to monitor the behavior. This group should include students and faculty, with prevention as the mission. Mandate that the school adopt a No-Bullying policy. Hang banners and posters in the school that promote awareness about bullying. Do trainings on what bullying is, its effects, and how to report it. Try to use videos, such as one I saw on ABC news, with Diane Sawyer, at http://www.youtube.com/watch?v=6Wcx2qM5C4g to make a lasting impact on kids, as long as this is age appropriate for kids watching. Create behavior improvement contracts and require bullies to sign them. Discourage bystander apathy by helping students understand why it is important to report bullying.

We must show our younger and adult kids what friendship is, and ensure they recognize bullying and know how to report it.

You want your child to develop healthy relationships. Use video modeling, role-play, social stories, and scripting to do this. Make sure your child's IEP reflects a No-Bullying policy.

The Profile of a Bully

Bullies do not act the same way friends do. Their intent is to harm. Bullies form unequal relationships. They enjoy feeling superior and want to be in control.

Bullies may humiliate, intimidate, threaten, or possibly physically harm their victims. They will threaten further aggression if they think you will report what they are doing to you.

Bullies internalize anger. They are jealous and resentful. Usually when confronted, they will deny the accusations.

Bullies are very adept at sizing up their victims.

Typical bully victims are kids with low self-esteem, the physically weak or frail, kids with disabilities, loners, kids that don't have friends, and kids who are anxious. However, any child can be a bully target.

The Teacher's Role

Educators must stand up to bullying. Teachers need to praise positive behavior, not ask questions like, "Who started this?", or ask victims if they said, "Stop." Teachers must adopt a zero-tolerance policy for any type of bullying. Offer the bully alternatives and praise him if he changes or complies. Remember you want to teach, and bullying makes teaching difficult. It is important to report a fellow teacher if he permits kids to bully others when he or she is in charge, or bullies any student.

Financial Bullying at Any Age

Children and adults with autism tend to be easy prey for financial bullying. In school, bullies may demand money or force the child to buy them food, sodas, CDs and other items. In many instances, they simply take what they want. Bullies run away with cash, sneakers, jewelry, keepsakes, and lunch.

It's a good idea to have a 'neurotypical' kid buddy up with your child. This can help prevent theft and abuse, and at the very least, ensure reporting to your school staff. Do not allow your child to take expensive things to school. Put his name on all items. Teach him to say, "NO! This is mine!" The sad truth is that kids are sometimes unable to communicate, scared or embarrassed, and/or intimidated.

When your child graduates, bullying doesn't end. Investment scams and pyramid schemes plague adults with autism. The workplace is notorious for manipulation and abuse. One news story reported that a co-worker bullied a person with autism into memorizing, and giving him, the combination to the safe. Later, the bully returned to work and robbed the safe.

Cyber Bullying

Your child is doing homework on the computer, when suddenly hundreds of Instant Messages arrive from kids at school. They banded together to bully your child online. The messages say things like, "You're retarded," "You're ugly," or "You're disgusting."

Technology makes cyber bullies feel safe. Cyber bullies seem to have more bravado and more brutality. Now, our children are no longer safe, even in their own home, unless you know about this and intervene.

These bullies will use emails, IMs, blogs, chat rooms or web pages to harass their victims. They can plot online to attack your child when he arrives at school, spread vicious rumors, set up an embarrassing website, reveal vulnerable information about autism, or send sensitive pictures of your child over the Internet. Many girls on the spectrum receive messages with sexual innuendos or suggestions.

So what can you do? Monitor your child's use of the computer and report online abuse immediately to the police. This will open a criminal complaint with computer trail. The computer-stored info can help punish or expel the bully. Remind your child often that he did not cause this. Research news articles and books on bullying. One excellent book is called, *The Bully, The Bullied, and the Bystander* by Barbara Coloroso. Once you realize that bullying can be so violent, and the victims can even commit suicide as a result, you'll see how important it is that you keep current on this subject. Teach your child to stand up for himself, report a situation, and be proud of reporting the incident. You must also show your child how to report the incident discretely so as not to create additional problems..

Bully Myths

There are as many myths about bullying as there are about autism. In both cases, if one embraces these misconceptions as truth it can be potentially harmful to our children:

You are a "sissy" or "rat" if you report bullying. Reporting a bullying incident may very well put an end to it for your child and others. Reporting can save other kids from getting bullied and it is the humane thing to do.

Bullies are terribly insecure. Actually, they are aggressive, cruel and lack empathy for others. They intend to hurt people, and while they may be 'insecure' this does not excuse their behavior.

Just ignore it, and it will go away! Bullies crave control, and they will pursue until they get what they want.

They only pick on kids with physical differences. No, they seek out everyone and anyone, including the weak, sensitive, and isolated. News reports and mental health statistics show that girls are especially skilled at going for the 'emotional jugular' (most sensitive issues for any kids).

Most incidents will occur outside of school. Statistics show that bullying takes place in hallways, lunchrooms, and the classroom. These incidents usually go unreported or unrecognized.

Just stand up for yourself and the bully will fold. Easy enough to say, but difficult to do, because most kids can't face down bullies.

Bullying is a small problem, statistically. Like dismal autism statistics, the National Institutes of Health, Centers for Disease Control and many other large government or university organizations report increasing numbers of bullies and bullying mental health issue results on a regular basis. Many kids even switch schools to get away from an abusive situation.

Many studies show that as many as half of the kids in school are bullied and there seems to be little difference between urban, suburban and rural areas.

All forms of bullying take their toll on the victim and can lead to depression, low self-esteem, and other issues that can last a lifetime. Get help for your child if he or she is bullied.

At age 11, Karen's son, Jonny wrote this letter to his bus driver, after being expelled from riding the bus for cutting the seat. Jonny was allowed to ride the bus again after his bus driver read this letter.

Dear Pat,

I am sorry for the seat, but I got angry because of Nicholas, because he's annoying me sometimes (99.9% of the time he is), and he's on the first bus I get on to go to school. He throws leftover chocolate Jell-O™ Pudding (in a container with holes on the lid) at me when he's getting off, and it gets my clothes dirty (mom doesn't want me to wear dirty clothing). While he's on, he and his friend gang up on me, and they move from seat to seat to get at me! They move ahead, one pair of seats at a time, bonk me on the head, and rush back to their seat. And sometimes, still in their seats, they throw assorted junk at me (Jell-O™ Pudding, paper balls, etc.) sometimes they miss.

He sometimes says I live in a garbage dump, a cardboard box, and on certain times he calls me "gay lord," gay not meaning happy. Matt told me to say, "Gee, thanks, I'll remember that!" when Nicholas says I am a gay lord. He sometimes swears. The one kid I saw and liked in his family was Nicholas' kid brother! Since I can only sit in the 4th seat or farther up, I'm a supreme target. Fortunately, they have never stolen my lunch yet.

The reason I made those holes was because I needed to do something to release my tension. My aide and I talked about what I could do instead of damaging other people's stuff.

Sincerely,
Jonny

Chapter 12

Puberty and Sexuality

Chapter 12
Puberty and Sexuality
Bill Davis

...that our children can progress toward having a relaxed mind and an open heart...
—Carolyn T. Bruey

When any child enters puberty, medical science proves they are up against surging hormones, growth spurts, sprouting hair, mood swings, and possible acne. Their bodies grow and change at alarming rates, so this is a very complex and difficult time. Teens with autism have sensory and behavioral issues that complicate puberty even more.

In addition, some doctors say that kids with autism may have small (petit mal) seizures, which, if not detected, may lead to things like aggression, self-injury, tantrums, and outbursts. You may want to have your child evaluated for these, be on the lookout for regression and the loss of cognitive gains.

During puberty, the hormonal change makes our children ultra sensitive and aggressive. Life becomes more socially demanding, and the social cues, already troublesome for some of our kids, are even subtler. If your child asks you a sensitive question, answer with honesty and don't change the subject. Talk with your physician about whether or not your child can benefit from medication, under very careful medical supervision, and you may want family counseling.

Sex Education and Explaining Sexuality

Some parents believe that developmental delays inhibit the onset of sexual feelings, and this may not be true. Your child may have sexual desires, so keep the discussions honest, and ensure your sure child understands.

Some Points on Sexuality to Discuss with Your Child:

Define and explain all private parts and their function. Stress the importance of cleanliness. Use pictures, anatomically correct dolls, or social stories. How about role-play?

Masturbation: Teach your child that pleasuring oneself in public is inappropriate, but is acceptable in private. Explain what masturbation is and why the climax occurs. Keep an eye out for the use of hard objects or excessive masturbation. You want to keep your child safe so that this does not turn into ritualistic, self-injurious behavior.

Set firm guidelines so your child does not get into compromising situations. Let your child know where it is acceptable to be naked. Repeat the lesson of "good touch" and "bad touch." Reinforce who is allowed to touch him, undress him, or dry him off after bathing. Set limits on self-touching and insure your child knows that it is inappropriate to touch others in their private areas. Empower your child by allowing him to be in a safe, private environment like your home bathroom, when he seems to need 'that special moment.' Educate your child about sexual responsibility. Teach birth control.

Don't use idiomatic language. Please say penis, not 'wiener' or 'peter.' Use concrete, natural language, and be age appropriate and simple. Do not engage in intricate, obscure descriptions.

Teach both girls and boys about menstruation, shaving, deodorant, pregnancy, needs, abuse, and gynecological exams.

Your doctor will tell you that medications can affect the sex drive, so ask your doctor about all possible side effects of the medications your child takes. In addition, keep data on these effects as they relate to your individual child.

If your teenager feels left out or alienated during puberty, teach him not to use sex as a way to become part of the 'in crowd'.

Parent Tip: The sexual preferences and desires of people with autism are as diverse as the disorder itself. Be accepting and loving. Observe and educate.

Sociability

Sociability is a very difficult topic. We long for our children to fit in, and yet we worry about how they will handle things when they become socially involved. Social situations are very trying for people with autism. Friendships are difficult to maintain, social banter is new territory, and dating is uncharted ground. Social interaction is frightening enough, but when compounded with speech and language difficulties, the inability to read social cues, and problems with body language, our children's social lives can become unbearable situations.

We always fear that our child will become the brunt of the joke, say the wrong thing, or put herself in danger. Sometimes your child may, unknowingly, commit a social blunder and you'll want to offer alternatives if you see or hear of this happening.

Fitting in

Most of us remember what being excluded feels like. It hurts. It is so hard when you are different. We all want friends, we all want to fit in, and we all want love. Unfortunately, we are sometimes faced with cruelty and rejection. Our children function differently. They try so hard to belong, and yet usually don't possess the skills to fit in. They may talk incessantly about one subject or categorize everything they see. This makes your child appear aloof, self-involved, or not interested. There are many sensory issues to deal with too, as your child may have weak musculature, poor coordination, or no interest in athletics. (See chapter 6 for visual therapies for coordination and improving sports performance.)

A mentor can help your child feel more comfortable in social groups by learning the rules and how to adjust. Exercise and fitness are important because working out helps self-esteem, opens avenues for communication, and may be a good way to meet new people.

Dating

Dating is uncharted territory. It is scary due to the subtleties. Everyone can benefit from dating guidance, so include this as you teach your child. You will also want to respect that some people with autism do not want to date. Here is some advice to share with your child with autism who is dating:

Like everything else we teach and re-teach, we pretty much have to break all things down to their simplest form and teach them, step by step as follows: Having similar interests or hobbies will put people at ease and allow for easy conversation. Sharing computer skills and interests is a great place to start. Parents need to help with dating by screening potential partners, picking safe meeting places, and dissecting dating "do's and don'ts."

Some good areas to meet a prospective date are study groups, the library, clubs, and places of worship.

Persons with autism find it very difficult to read social cues and body language, all the tools we rely on when we are out on a date. Therefore, our kids are starting out at a deficit.

Tell your child not to presume that someone is interested in him, just because he is attracted to that person. Help him recognize subtleties. Does that girl like me? Does she want to go out again? Is it getting serious? Use social stories, educational videos, movies, and act out scenarios before your child dates.

This section is for the person with autism.

For the person with autism, dating can develop into a hurtful and embarrassing experience.

A date does not have to develop into a serious relationship. It doesn't have to lead to anything. Relax and enjoy your time out together.

If the date does start to turn into a relationship, you might want to reveal your disorder and behavioral cues. Talk to the person honestly and openly about yourself and your (for lack of a better word) "idiosyncrasies." Prepare them and let them know what to expect.

Remember, communication is the key. Talk to your date, to your parents, to your mentor, and to your counselor. Do not rush "touching." It will come naturally. Once again, communicate with your partner.

Discuss your interests but try not to perseverate or focus on one topic. Dominating the date with a discussion of every race car driver's number and colors can make for a long and boring time. Let the other person talk as well.

If you find yourself in a group, watch the typical people. You can take some dating cues from them. Be yourself but avoid acting stereotypical. There are times when you have to imitate others to get through the day. There are also moments when you just have to disguise your disorder. It is the cost of living in a society.

Typical people see lack of eye contact as being deceitful, so try hard to maintain some level of eye contact. Smile, talk casually, and don't ask a lot of personal questions. Be subtle, respectful, and mind the boundaries of personal space.

During conversations, answer questions honestly but don't give out too much personal information.

Look at yourself in the mirror. What does your image reflect? Are you dressed similarly to your peers? Is your hygiene up to par?

Don't stare at your date or speak about past boyfriends or girlfriends.

If you are invited to a party or gathering, don't be the first to arrive. This way you will not "stick out," and you will have time to familiarize yourself with what's going on. How are people talking? What groups are they in? Do you know anyone?

If you really like someone, please don't tell everyone about your attraction. They may bully you or turn the situation against you.

Your visual skills can help with dating. Picture the date, how it will go, and use visual images to understand possible challenging situations

If you enter into a serious relationship, avoid the negative people in your life. Bullies will "attack" if they sense you are happy and satisfied.

Tell your special friend that they can feel free to question you about autism. Explain how they can help if you are overloaded or agitated.

It may be very difficult but try to be spontaneous. Don't prepare lists or schedules. If you are enjoying your time at dinner, then let it continue. Do not be too strict with time.

Women may find dating a little easier. A man with autism who is introverted is looked upon as weak or lacking confidence, but shyness is perceived as a good quality in a woman. In all probability, men will approach you. This saves you from the awkwardness of asking someone out on your own.

Do not focus on details. Keep your dating rules simple.

Keep up your confidence and self-esteem.

Sexual Abuse

Women with disabilities are abused at alarming rates. The U. S. Department of Justice says that more than half of women with developmental disabilities will be sexually assaulted during their lifetime. Women with autism in institutions are particularly vulnerable. If abused they remain silent. When the assault is finally revealed, the police will invariably question why the crime was not reported immediately. They ask: "Did she say no?" "Why wasn't she upset?"

Children with developmental disabilities are abused more than children without disabilities, according to a U. S. Department of Justice report.

Our children may not have the language to express abuse that has occurred. Parents take heed; our children are sexual beings and must be educated and protected. Be prepared. Use your intuition and realize that some situations might be uncomfortable for you.

To help your child develop a positive self-image, show him how good he looks in the mirror, and help him to realize how he looks to the world. Many parents allow their kids to dress independently, and they abide by their child's choices. There is value to this philosophy, but you have to step in if your child appears vulnerable or is dressing provocatively. People with autism can be easily manipulated, and we have seen how they can be bullied.

People with autism sometimes will possess weak self-help skills, immature social skills, and the inability to report incidents or defend themselves. They often have poor judgment, but have the desire to please others. They lack social dependency and physical strength. Naiveté is a typical characteristic.

Some abusers think people with autism have no feelings, and therefore they are not affecting their psyche. Predators and bullies will cunningly draw our children in. They are also adept at oppressing our kids.

In the case of talking with your child about possible sexual abuse, go with your gut and follow the trail of clues. If your child seems changed or embarrassed, this could be a red flag. Encourage your child to communicate with you. Speak clearly, concisely, and use a normal level of volume and tone of voice. Do not suggest scenarios, but take your child's testimony seriously. Assure him it is perfectly acceptable and right to tell. Tell your child he or she is not to blame, and that autism is not to blame.

Ask open-ended questions: "What was done to you?" Repeat the last part of the sentence. A specific question would be more like: "Did he touch you here?" Ask all the "W" questions: Who, what, when, where. Our children may be confused with the time things may have occurred, so use association. "Did this happen at the time you usually watch the 'Sesame Street' show?"

A medical exam is necessary, not just for proof but for sexually transmitted diseases, injuries, and pregnancy. If a crime has been committed, contact the police. Disclose your child's disorder and his method of communication. Assure the child that he did nothing wrong, that's not why you are talking to the police. Make him feel comfortable and protected. If it goes to trial, consider getting permission to videotape your child's testimony. This will keep him or her from becoming overstimulated in a crowded courtroom and will prevent seeing the accused face to face.

Let your loved one know he can question authority. Blindly obeying authority can put our children in compromising positions.

Teach the child with autism about locker room behavior. Let him know about the "code," privacy, and potential practical jokes.

Make a list of different types of sexual abuse, such as unwelcome sexual contact, inappropriate touching and date rape and date rape drugs. If the person with autism is intimate with their partner, then forcing different types of sex play on them is considered abuse. Sexual abuse is often accompanied by threats and physical harm. Use videos, video modeling, role-play, social stories, and generalization. Some general red flags are bruising, scratches, acting out, outbursts, overt sexual behavior, depression, and urinating in inappropriate places. We know that people with developmental delays are victimized at a much higher rate than the rest of the population. Persons with autism who have experienced sexual abuse usually live in silence. They deserve privacy and respect. We must educate, guide, and empower them.

Hygiene

Here is some advice on how to teach washing, brushing, bathing, etc. Good books are available on personal habits and hygiene. Once again, you are the parent, so be intuitive.

Hygiene is like fitness. They both promote health, self-esteem, and a sense of one's body. Early on, establish routines for cleanliness and health. Taking care of one's body provides a feeling of independence. Hygiene becomes even more important as our kids get older because their bodies change so radically, with "more to groom" and new odors to deal with.

Create simple, concise hygienic routines. Teach modesty as well, as this comes in very handy during puberty.

Here are some items you can put on your lists as reminders for your child:

With the numerous hygiene requirements that accompany adolescence, many families make a morning and bedtime list, such as brushing teeth, hair care, skin care, fingernail care, wearing clean clothing, showering, and deodorant. Adolescents will also have some new items to contend with, such as cleaning up after sports and trimming public hair such as underarm, facial and leg hair. They will be dealing with cologne and perfume, acne, bras and menstrual hygiene as well.

Educate your child about not touching people who are bleeding or blood on surfaces. Many children are fascinated with cuts or scrapes, so make sure that they doesn't carry over that fascination to others and touch the wounds and scabs of strangers. Also, educate about not touching public water fountains spouts to the mouth.

Label the products your child can use, and those that were not for him or are potentially harmful. Some parents initially use a lot of "hand over hand" with prompts, and then move to using verbal commands. Try to keep things consistent, like having the toothbrush always the same color, products the same and all placed in the same area.

Hygiene is not just about health and safety; it is about self-esteem and personal strength. Cleanliness shows others you care about yourself. Teach your children about hygiene to show that you care about them.

Different, Special Doctor's Visits

It is common for doctors to say to boys or men, "Turn your head and cough," As our children develop physically at the same rate as typically developing children, we cannot put off these very important exams, as they are very necessary for our children's health and physical safety.

Males will have their genitals and scrotum examined. The aforementioned coughing allows the doctor to evaluate for hernias and tumors. Take the time to demonstrate to your son what will occur during the doctor's visit. If your son seems confused, demonstrate, turn your head and cough, and say, "Do this!" so he can follow suit. Talk about semen, and explain what might come out of his penis after masturbation or even during the night.

Stay in the examination room with your child. The dreaded prostate exam has to be discussed. Some children require an enema to help with their bowel movements. It can be awfully invasive. Be reassuring and talk about privacy and trust. Let the doctor know if your child is sensitive to noise or lights. If your child is very tactile, explain the best way to approach him. When presenting your strategies, consider all behavioral issues. Mention seizures and regression. Comfort and educate your child.

Talk to the doctor and let him know what precautions to take so that your child feels comfortable. The physician should come across as very caring. The doctor must remain calm and accommodating. Keep the lighting low. Discuss your strategies with the doctor beforehand. If he is going to discuss sexual behavior with your child, then discuss your sexual values with him. Reveal what your child knows about sex. Use the correct medical terms with your child and discuss strategy with the doctor. He may use visual aids or model the behavior. Train the doctor to develop the ability to communicate with your child. Ask your pediatrician to recommend a doctor who is familiar with autism.

Women's exams are complicated, frightening, and sometimes painful, especially gynecological exams. Bleeding can occur. Map the entire gynecological exam, including breast exams and pap smears. Women with autism must have gynecological examinations with the same frequency as other women, for health, proper development, and abuse. The doctor and parent must discuss birth control and safe sex with sexually active women.

What about self-examinations? Boys are urged to examine testicles for lumps beginning at age fifteen, and girls to check their breasts. The parent can easily self-model, and then show the teenager how to do it him or herself.

If you are taking your daughter for her exam, there are many points to discuss with the doctor. Just getting on the examination table can be a sensory nightmare. Explain the stirrups and the speculum. Discuss all tactile issues. Even the room's air conditioning system can throw our children off. The doctor must tell your daughter what he or she is doing every step of the way. Explore alternative methods. Some positions do not require stirrups and the swab can be inserted without using the speculum. Ask your daughter if she wants a female or male doctor. Plan this visit well and walk your child through it.

Chapter 13

Issues for Boys with Autism

Chapter 13
Issues for Boys with Autism

Editor's Note: There are some explicit sections in Chapter 13. You may want to decide whether they are appropriate for your child to read.

...they also light the way to such love...

—Andrew Solomon

The Issues

Many men tell me that they long for an athletic son, who will be the captain of the football team. They also tell me they want their boy to grow up knowing how to fix cars and excuse the wording here, but also know how to 'make the ladies swoon'. While times are changing, I still hear that dads want their sons to be "tough."

Interestingly, I believe that all our kids with autism are tough. Imagine boys like my Chris, sitting through forty hours of ABA (Applied Behavioral Analysis) a week? Who else can continue striving and growing in a world that is foreign and hurtful? Who else could manage to laugh with their Dad while their intestines scream with pain? However, our boys have developed a new kind of "tough." They are sensitive, ethereal beings, who are even poetic in their attempt to achieve harmony with the world. I am jealous.

Most reports say that boys are four times more likely than girls to have autism. In my experience however, girls with autism have to deal with more problems. I think we expect more from them, and tragically, they seem to be sexually abused more often. I know their "feminine" medical issues are overwhelming. I'll address this in the next chapter.

According to a study in the journal, Neuroscience, (Neuroscience, July 19, 2006, 26(29):7674-7679), David Amaral and Cynthia Mills Shuman of the University of California, Davis, say that males with autism have fewer neurons in their amygdale. The amygdale are two, almond shaped masses of gray matter, which are part of the limbic system.

While this information is medically complex, and has both emotional and learning consequences, for discussion purposes, it is possible that fewer neurons make boys less fearful in situations where they might otherwise need that emotion for protective purposes. It could hold a key to understanding aggression also.

Boys with autism also have higher levels of growth hormones compared to boys who do not have autism. Researchers from the National Institutes of Health (NIH), Centers for Disease Control and Prevention, and the Cincinnati Children's Hospital, speculate that this could account for the larger head circumference recorded in boys with autism. It could also have something to do with why boys weigh more, although we don't know for sure. The study concludes that boys are not just growing faster, but certainly, there is far more going on in boys with autism than we know.

Men in Institutions and Group Homes
Bill Davis

At a recent seminar sponsored by The Center for Developmental Disabilities at Temple University, the advocate who presented brought a film about boys with autism living in an institution in the 1950s. He said that this movie was filmed in secrecy. The young men were wearing nothing but large, white diapers. Their rooms were stark, with no color, no toys, and no pictures. They slept on metal cots, often chained to their beds, washed down with a hose, and fed through a trough. These boys all demonstrated severe autistic characteristics such as hand flapping, head banging, eye gouging, and chewing on everything in sight. One boy was sitting in his own feces, eating a mop head.

Institutionalization can be a nightmare for a non-verbal person with weak self-help skills, and a host of sensory issues. Early on, many people with autism lived in institutions from diagnosis until their death. They did not get any type of training, nor an education. When the suffering and deplorable conditions were finally exposed, these institutions were forced to close. Many men with autism were simply 'dropped off' into the community. They did not fare well. Some were herded off like cattle into group settings which lacked preparedness and training. Their average life span, after being dismissed from the institution, was sixty-two days! They were not ready to deal with self-care, the community, or life in general.

Institutional Life Must Be Updated

In today's world, our institutions for those with autism, or any challenge, must include activities, education and training. This means things like trips into the neighborhood, exercise, and health care. Building self-worth must be a priority.

When institutions reigned supreme in the United States during the 1960s, many children were assigned to state facilities. The attitude toward persons with developmental disabilities was radically different. Many families were ashamed, and it was common for a physician to advise a family to institutionalize immediately, because he or she believed that the parents could not handle a disabled child. If you saw the recent HBO special, *Temple Grandin*, you'll know exactly how autism was perceived, and what a parent had to do to in order to advocate for a better life for their child. If you did not see this special, I recommend that you rent it.

You will also want to know what I've been told about sexual assaults in institutions. Just as in our prison systems, males with autism, living in institutions, are sexually assaulted on a regular basis. Statistics on this are difficult to obtain, but anecdotal evidence is strong. I am told the boys or men suffer in silence. Men aren't supposed to acquiesce, so they may be embarrassed to admit that they have been assaulted. Many are non-verbal, adding to the problem. Their assaulters assure them that this is normal behavior. Sometimes the abuser will provide privileges or gifts, which confuses the inmate/patient. Patients fear if they report the incident, they won't get the care they need anymore. They are afraid of physical retribution. If they do report they may not be taken seriously or believed, as some in charge don't think boys or men with autism are sexually active, so the abuse couldn't happen.

Institutions can be very abrasive and punishing. People with autism must learn to think for themselves and believe in who they are. Managing life on a daily basis is difficult for our children, but, in my opinion, that should not condemn them to life in an institution.

Every one of us has different talents, and we all contribute to society in different ways.

Given all that I said above, we do have some wonderful group homes, institutions and psychiatric centers, with trained personnel, treatment plans, and community-based programs today. If you do decide to institutionalize your child, check the facility's reputation and ensure they have a comprehensive and humane program.

Comments About Autism Tomorrow
Dr. Stephen Shore

In the world of autism tomorrow, I would like to see more emphasis on people with autism and their contributions to society, and I believe we are headed in this direction.

In addition, I'd like to see part of the curriculum in grade school through college, include meaningful study about the differences between boys and girls, as well as the diversity in people both on and off the autism spectrum. There will hopefully be exploration and discussion as to the particular strengths and challenges each student and each teacher faces, as well as how to focus on how to best ways employ one's strengths, leading to fulfilling and productive lives. Those who now have autism or other "disabilities," will be referred to as individuals who have greater diversity within the usual set of skills.

I can only pray that there will be a greater understanding regarding social interaction. The person who speaks deeply about a subject, with little eye contact and not much introduction beforehand, will be valued just as much as the one making good eye contact and following the rules we have set up now.

Finally, I hope to see the condition of autism referred to as an expression of the diversity in the human gene pool. Interventions in the educational, behavioral, developmental, sensory integration, and biomedical areas will be employed to help those with autism lead fulfilling and productive lives, irrespective of their differences.

Chapter 14

Issues for Girls with Autism

Chapter 14
Issues for Girls with Autism

There is little research on girls with autism. One reason may be the belief that boys with autism outnumber girls with autism by about four to one. Most research is done on the boys and researchers conclude, as they do in many medical studies, that the findings must be the same for the girls.

...occasionally, I crack open a door to the future...

—Shannon Johnson

We've discovered, as you will see in Ruth's comments at the end of this chapter, that the diagnosis of girls with autism seems to slip under the radar screen during the early years. When girls with autism are young, they seem to fit in socially better than their male counterparts. In addition, even though they may have severe sensory issues, they don't seem to throw tremendous tantrums or experience intense outbursts like boys do.

It's difficult enough for 'neurotypical' girls to fit into the secret world of teenage girls, but here are some additional challenges that girls with autism face:

- Trying to keep up with hidden agendas, colloquial conversations, and quick communications, such as cell phone texting.

- Group acceptance, with the societal expectations that girls need to be pretty, perfect and feminine.

- Breaking into tight-knit social groups, with a well-known female hierarchy, and which many studies show are typically unforgiving.

- Striving for independence with very weak self-help skills.

Left out of the social circle, these girls are ostracized and ridiculed. They tend to have trouble dressing like the others, and suffer more than the other girls with a vast array of complications during their menstrual cycles.

Here's some advice for dealing with the menstrual cycles of girls with autism:

- Remind your daughter to remove her tampon or pad. Girls with autism find it very hard to remember this task. Leave reminder notes or mark it on a calendar.

- Try junior size tampons before introducing the regular size. Many girls reject pads because they're too bulky.

- Many girls feel "dirty" during their menstrual cycle and their sensory issues rise. Be aware that their feelings are amplified a thousand fold. They must contend with tampons, raging hormones, bloating, and mood swings.

- Electric razors seem best for shaving. They are safer, and creams which remove hair, tend to have offensive odors.

As girls with autism get older, their "meltdowns" tend to be dismissed out of hand, blaming her because she is a girl, or is just having her period. Instead of an autism label, girls are often tagged with being over dramatic, ultra sensitive, cranky, and irritable. They enter adulthood, in many cases, as social outcasts who are depressed, have never dated, and flit from job to job.

Adult women with autism continue to have a very difficult time fitting in socially. They become extremely depressed, and sometimes suicidal.

Parent Tip: If you have a girl, recognize they are often treated differently than boys.

Women in Institutions and Group Homes

According to Temple University Center on Disabilities, the abuse of women with disabilities in institutions is horrific and out of control. Because most assaults go unreported, we have little data on these women.

Millions of women, worldwide, are disabled. We know that women with disabilities experience higher rates of violence than the general female population, and this seems to bear true in women in institutions.

Here is some information I know to be true firsthand, of girls and women in institutions, and you may want to do more research yourself.

- Many girls suffer forced abortions and sterilizations, and may have to give up their sexual and reproductive rights when institutionalized

- Women with autism are extremely vulnerable when residing in an institutional setting, and are at greater risk of maltreatment than any other population

- Sometimes girls cannot speak to defend themselves, or worse, they do not know if a crime has been committed against them

- Those who can communicate, may fear retribution and the denial of care for speaking up.

- Women with disabilities are the most likely to be institutionalized than any other group

Women with autism need a voice! You can help by researching institutions for girls and women with autism and speaking out publicly, if you find injustices.

Growing From A Girl into A Woman With Autism
Ruth E. Snyder, RN

I am now thirty-ish. I realized something was wrong as a child, but it was especially obvious when I was pre-teen. I did not know much about autism before my diagnosis in my early thirties and often wonder why I was not diagnosed as a young girl.

As an adult, when I first started embracing my diagnosis of autism, a few very important people in my life helped me survive and grow. They kept me from falling into that place of denial that had become commonplace for me. One mother of another adult with autism, helped me begin to pull together the threads of my past, and find a way to mend and hem the fabric, so there were not as many loose threads.

When I first told people I have autism, they would make one of four statements. The first was, "You can't be autistic." The rest were that they were sure I wasn't because I could make eye contact, speak, and of course, I am a girl. These are the stereotypical social norms and expectations. Can you see me banging my head now?

When someone would say this to me, it hurt because it felt like they were calling me a liar, right to my face. Women have emotions, autistics don't, and when I was stereotyped, it tempted me to bang my head once again. Instead of head banging, I would bring these issues to my surrogate mother and my physician. He kindly pointed out that if they were calling anyone a liar, it was he, since he diagnosed it.

I began to realize that I was taught to believe my problems in society were gender-based. I was a woman living in a man's world, and I learned to work with it. Looking back, I also remember how often I thought it was easier to take on the traditional male role of provider and protector, than it was trying to be a woman. Choosing an education and a career path, which was structured, would have been easier for me. The rules were clear, and I would not need much social interaction. However, when I chose traditional female roles or jobs, i.e., server, store cashier, or nurse, the game changed. Over the past decade, I realized how happy as I am with my life as a woman if for no other reason than the fact that I have given birth, something men cannot do or experience.

Finding female role models and mentors was a challenge after my diagnosis discovery, so I decided to look outside of the autism box and into the world we often call 'neurotypical'. I also remained connected with autistic women all over the world, on the Internet, or at conferences. It felt safe to be social networking and demonstrating good social skills with women that get it.

The more I researched autism from a logical and professional perspective, the more I understood the stereotypical judgments, opinions, and even approaches to treatment. I began to understand the confusions of neurotypicals and people with autism. Since autism is a developmental disability, I wondered, maybe feared, that it would be impossible for me to ever mature. That is when I realized that I skipped several 'neurotypical' developmental stages that 'neurotypical' girls naturally tend to do. I realized this by watching my daughter grow into a woman, and I wanted to learn to embrace being a girl, so I can mature to be a woman, too.

When my daughter chose to become a U.S. Marine, I recognized her need to learn to be that strong woman, the role model she admired so much. I supported it, and even wanted to go through it with her, because it sounded like a fun job, one which I had never considered. The night of her prom is the only time I had doubts about joining her. She pulled together the most amazing outfit and hairstyle, but when she needed help with her makeup, I had to call the neighbor. My daughter was helping me with fashion and decorating, and I finally understood I was missing not only the genetic ability, but also lacked the social network to learn such things.

My daughter was always more of a girl than I ever wanted to be. Fate, luck, her 'neurotypical' traits, paternal family influence, will, genetics, and her spirit have all helped her when I could not.

There are so many gender-specific aspects about me, that I look at from my past with wonder, just waiting to know the answers. Questions about why I cannot learn to be a domestic diva, happy homemaker, fashionable, trendy, giggle with girls, cry at movies that move me emotionally, or laugh at things other women often find funny or socially correct, actually plague me. Maybe this is why I have the drive and desire to share my insights with others. I know there are as many answers as there are questions that need asking.

The more I embrace the feminine energy and gifts, the more I respect the male species, and understand women I once had no clue about. The more I embrace the autistic traits and challenges, the more connected I feel to other people, the stronger the empathy and the emotions for others. Sometimes the emotions are too much to manage. Sometimes, the response is opposite. I laugh when others would cry, and I cry when others would laugh. Now I understand why others see me very differently than I see myself.

Chapter 15

Financial Planning

Chapter 15
Financial Planning

Bill Davis, Kim Schnepper, Martin Cherrin, and John Dowson

...our efforts at advocacy have gained a voice nationally...

—Robert Naseef, Ph.D.

Editor's Note: This financial chapter comes with the usual disclaimers: See your attorney or certified financial specialist for advice and guidance. This chapter is for informational purposes only and not to be construed as financial advice.

Note to Canadian Citizens: Mr. John Dowson wrote a section at the end of this chapter, especially for you.

Most states will provide some services for children with autism, usually funded by various government programs, depending upon your child's needs.

A certified financial specialist and eldercare attorney can help guide you about these programs and your child's eligibility for them as well.

You may also want to contact your local Autism Society of America chapter to obtain more information about the developmental disabilities services in your community. Once a child is deemed eligible, he/she may be awarded service hours.

Many states have waiting lists for services, but some states provide services to everyone who qualifies. It is then up to the parent to choose a provider agency for each type of service. Speech therapists, occupational therapists, and physical therapists are in high demand, but most states pay only modest rates.

Thus, it can be a challenge to find them. Similarly, it can be very challenging to find home care providers and others you may need, but don't give up.

Some local agencies can train providers who will help you, as well as pay their fees.

School Programs

If your child is very young (generally under three), there are early intervention programs. For children over three years of age, pre-school and school programs are available. Parents should contact the local school district for information about local programs.

In some cases, you may want your child in a separate program for special needs children, but if your child is higher functioning, it's usually best to integrate into the regular school program, providing there is enough support, i.e., a part or full-time aide, and other accommodations as needed.

It is important that you work carefully with your child's teacher on an Individualized Education Program (IEP), which is discussed in more detail in Chapter 4. Additionally, meeting with your child's classmates and/or their parents, can be helpful in encouraging other students to interact positively with your child.

In some states, your school district, rather than the state, may fund home therapy programs such as ABA and speech therapy. However, it may take considerable effort to convince the school district to provide those services. Check with your local ASA chapter and other parents about how these services are usually provided in your state.

The Letter of Intent

The letter of intent is not necessarily a legal document, but a guide to your child's care. The document provides insight into the child's life and hopes for the future. It will describe your child's history and illustrate his daily routine. Update it on a frequent basis. The Letter of Intent will direct those involved in your child's life after you are gone.

This letter may be done in conjunction with a will, and again, your attorney or certified financial specialist will advise you about this.

This letter will save a lot of time. Family members and therapists will have a directive that provides crucial information on the routine, hopes and dreams you have for your child.

Contents of the Letter of Intent:

Once again, use an attorney to advise you on formal Letters of Intent, and for discussion purposes only, I am going to list some items I included in my Letter of Intent.

- History: medical, therapy, education, etc.
- Personality: likes and dislikes, problems, strengths, personal preferences, clothing, games, music, fitness
- Make a list of who should be contacted after your death.
- Housing: the best places for your child to reside
- Job training
- Behavioral needs
- Religion
- Recreation
- Daily routine
- Things your child enjoys at home

Let people know that this document exists. Perhaps you can store it on your computer so you can update it frequently and easily. Be specific and communicate clearly. This is your chance to lay the groundwork for your child's future. The Letter of Intent will provide a glimpse into the unique world of your child with autism.

Protecting Your Child's Assets

I am putting this section in to ensure that parents are well aware of what could happen to your child's assets. Take note and take care, and while these things happen, with excellent legal advice you may be able to avoid any or all of these. Just know that these things are possible.

We all have read countless stories of appointed trustees or guardians looting the holdings of the disabled. Accountants, lawyers, and even family members can invade, steal, and take full control of your child's assets. Our children are very vulnerable to these attacks. The situations and the laws are so complex that many states and judges are not prepared to deal with these issues. No real checks and balances seem to be in place.

The courts are overburdened, some judges uneducated on this issue, and laws may not be followed. Beware that some appointed guardians have the ability to request medications, which may keep their disabled clients uninvolved, so they are free to disperse funds at will.

That said; keep your child's IEPs and other evaluations handy. Clearly spell out who will make decisions when you are gone. Talk to siblings and relatives on a regular basis and let them know what is expected of them. Appoint successor guardians. Ensure that services will kick in immediately if you are ill or pass away.

George Carlin always said, "We don't pass away or expire, we die. Just say it!" Use support groups for resources and referrals. Start now to put line up all the proverbial ducks in a row. If you plan the transference of power and assets, then you are truly protecting your child.

Financial Planning
Kim Schnepper and Martin Cherrin

Note from Kim: People always ask why I have such a passion for the insurance industry and special needs planning. There are many reasons, but two stick out in my mind. 1) When I was eleven years old, I was diagnosed with epilepsy, and as a result, became ineligible for life insurance, disability and long-term care. 2) Growing up, I was fortunate to have an extremely loving and supportive family who set up trusts to help secure my future. The trusts were in my name, which not only left me extremely vulnerable to creditors, but left me ineligible for government benefits.

I want to make sure people don't experience the same problems I have. With the help of my colleagues, a strong network of lawyers, and accountants, I now help families by making sure a child's trust is not only set up properly, but funded properly; and if possible make sure that child gets insurance before somebody tells them, "No."

Financial Planning—Should I or Shouldn't I?

Finance and planning are two terms that have always worried people. However, after the market crash of October 2008, many people are scared or concerned about their future.

When your child has autism or is developmentally disabled, those concerns are intensified immensely with a constant worry about whether he or she will need assistance as an adult. If assistance is required, it is likely to be for a much longer period due to medical advancements and generally lengthening lifespan.

Is Special Needs Planning on Your "To Do List?"

When people dream of having children, they realize they will be their child's greatest asset. They also dream of their children becoming independent. However if your child has autism or is developmentally disabled, often parents are their child's greatest asset for life, at least to some degree. For these parents, planning for the future must immediately be added to the "To Do List." This chapter will provide a basic idea of what needs to be done and how to begin.

When parents don't set up a Special Needs Trust, it is generally for one of three reasons:

1. Time. All parents are busy, but the parent of a child with autism must constantly plan for the present, having to incorporate unique social situations and medical considerations, which can leave precious little time for long-range planning for them or their family.

2. Lack of knowledge. Not knowing where to begin, what the benefits of planning are, or the different options that may exist, are some of the areas that parents struggle with. Many people feel overwhelmed so they choose to do nothing..

3. Fear. Very often, the thought of not being there to help take care of a child can be crippling to parents so much so that they cannot bear to think about what their child's future will be when they are no longer able to care for their child. As a result, they don't make any formal plans, leaving their child extremely vulnerable.

Ensuring your child's future is secure can also be called estate planning. The term "estate planning" misleads people because it is a concept usually associated with people who are wealthy. However, no matter what your income, if you are the parent of a child with autism, or a developmental disability that will likely affect his or her independence as an adult, estate planning is essential.

Why plan?

The core goals of setting up a proper plan are fairly universal:

1.) Happiness and security for your son or daughter throughout his or her lifetime.

2.) Ensuring your child will be able to use all three pillars of support: family, government, and charities.

How Planning Ensures the Use of the Three Pillars, Pitfall Free

If your child has autism, he or she may need physical and emotional care throughout his or her life. There is no greater support than that of a loving family member.

When leaving care to another family member, there are many variables to consider.

- Will that person always be there?

- Does that family member have a family of his or her own, or intend to get married and/or have children?

- Is he or she financially stable?

With an appropriate plan in place, you can be assured:

- Money you set aside to help your child will be used for that purpose alone and can't be touched by divorce, lawsuits, or creditors.

- The person you choose to care for your child is financially equipped to do so.

The estate plan you choose can also integrate provisions for all family members, not just a child whom is developmentally disabled. This is done because each element of the plan affects the entire family.

Government Benefits

Our government has many programs your child can use. Estate planning for your developmentally disabled child is designed to incorporate these benefits into your child's life, without endangering them. However if you are unaware of the "fine print" of government funding, family support can be harmful.

A generous and loving grandparent, family member, or friend can inadvertently ruin an entire plan for a special needs child simply by leaving funds or assets directly to that child.

The most frequently used programs are Social Security, Supplemental Security Income, also referred to as SSI, and Medicaid.

- Social Security is an entitlement program based upon the earnings of the individual, or parents of the individual.

- Medicaid is a means-based program designed to help pay medical expenses.

- SSI is a federal program designed to supplement the income of the disabled. Many states will increase a person's SSI depending upon his or her financial status. The purpose is to provide means for shelter, clothing, and food. It is a means-based program, so if your child has more than two thousand dollars in his or her name, he or she is deemed ineligible. Another problem can be the misappropriation of funds by using it for purposes besides food, clothing, and shelter. When this occurs, a person's benefits will be reduced or eliminated, and SSI can ask for reimbursement.

If your child can qualify the programs can be very helpful, but not always easy to obtain. You have to make sure to know all of the rules, because it is extremely easy to stray and inadvertently break one of those rules, disallowing your son or daughter the benefits that he or she deserves. It is essential that you, all family members, caregivers, and close friends understand the "fine print" of government assistance programs.

Lee Chase is the Executive Director for The Dawn on Hope, a school in Tennessee for the intellectually or developmentally disabled. He told us a poignant story of a severely retarded boy who lost both parents in a car accident. Caring neighbors took up a collection, which raised over $10,000.

Afterwards, they deposited the money into a bank account in the child's name, bringing his assets above the cutoff limit for government aid. As a result, the child's benefits were terminated. Chase fought with the authorities for well over a year before the child's benefits were restored.

A client of mine has a nineteen-year-old son with autism. His grandmother put $17,000 in the child's name in a joint account with his parents, figuring they could use it to buy him a stereo, DVD player, etc. She was also about to leave him another $50,000, as he is a named beneficiary in her life insurance policy. This $17,000 left the young man ineligible for many government programs.

These are just two examples of what can happen when a person leaves assets directly in a disabled child's name. To avoid this problem, many people choose to put the funds and or assets intended for their disabled child's future in the name of a family member or caregiver. This plan is not foolproof. Parents run a risk that the legacy intended to leave their child will not be used for the reason intended. Some of the more common causes of this happening include divorce, bankruptcy, lawsuits, and general mismanagement for personal use.

Three Basic Estate Plans to Fund for Special Needs

These three basic estate plans provide for those with special needs, although the most efficient and problem-free is one designed for that purpose.

Plan #1: Leaving Assets in Your Child's Name.

Three options in which you can leave assets to your child:

Option A—Take assets and leave them outright to your child in his or her name.

Option B—Leave the assets to the child but have them managed by a guardian.

Option C—Place the assets in a trust. This trust directs the trustee to pay for the child's primary care needs. This is referred to as a nondiscretionary trust.

Pluses:

- If there are sufficient assets, your child may become financially independent.

Minuses:

- If assets are left in a child's name, he or she may be ineligible or disqualified from government programs. A developmentally disabled child might not qualify for a residential program if he or she is left assets to assist in his or her primary care. This could happen whether the child is in a guardianship or in a nondiscretionary trust, or holds the funds outright.

- Depending on the overall plan, other children may be disinherited in the attempt to move sufficient assets to provide for the lifetime care of the special needs child. Disinheriting other children is not an acceptable option for many families.

Plan #2: Disinheriting Your Child.

Should you choose not to make provisions for your child for after you die, you must understand this means nothing is transferred to the child outright, in guardianship or trust. By disinheriting the child completely, he or she would be eligible for most government programs.

The government will provide the child's primary care and the remaining family may informally assist the child. However, assistance should not include contributions for primary care as the government could invoke its reimbursement or offset rules.

Pluses:

- You can be confident that your son and daughter will be eligible for whichever government assistance programs are in place.
- You don't have to worry about disinheriting other family members in order to create a plan for your child's futures.

Minuses:

- By leaving the government as the sole guarantor of your child's care, you leave a lot to chance because you don't know what those programs will be like in 1, 5, 10, or 20 years from now or if they will still exist.
  - Will they be adequate?

- Will your child be able to see the top specialists?

- What happens if your child is independent, but still needs help?

In Plan #2, there is little if any certainty as to the results. A key to estate planning is establishing a plan where the parents' wishes, desires, and goals will be carried out. Most people aren't willing to take that risk.

Plan #3: Setting Up a Special Needs Trust.

A Special Needs Trust is one in which assets are not directly in your child's name. It gives the appearance that you have disinherited your child, as a result he or she should qualify for government and charitable programs.

These programs provide for the child's primary care. This trust will use, control, and distribute funds to a child to provide any additional expenses. This is the most efficient and problem-free plan.

A Special Needs Trust could be set up to provide improved medical care or residential care. For instance, if the government medical program provided for the payment of one medical opinion, the trustee might pay for a second opinion.

In Plan #3, all three pillars of support (the government, charity, and family) work together. The child receives primary care from government and charity resources. The family sets up trust that is used to supplement the benefits being received.

Funding the Special Needs Trust

Special Needs Trust can be funded by annuities or life insurance, although the latter is vastly more common and flexible. Following are three options:

1. An insurance policy to be owned by one or both of the parents, naming the trust as beneficiary. A Will could establish the trust. This is called a testamentary trust.

2. A revocable living trust established by the parents during their lifetime.

3. The policy is owned by and payable to an irrevocable trust.

The final part of estate planning that is very key, to decide how the assets are to be divided among your other children, spouse and yourself. Many people forget this, and the end result isn't always pretty. You can't assume that if you have more than one child that he or she will be okay with the fact that the assets aren't divided equally.

How Much Money Is Needed?

Deciding this figure involves financial calculations that include the projections of how much money will be needed for all family members, not just the expenses of a developmentally disabled child.

When doing this, it is best to leave government assistance programs out, because you don't know whether or not your son or daughter will be eligible, or whether or not the program will still be in existence.

Equally important is deciding on when that money will be needed. For instance, will there be a significant financial burden at the death of the father or mother, or both? On the other hand, is the family in a financially secure position with no significant issues unless both parents have died?

Finally, choices have to be made between the purchase of a Whole Life Policy or Term Policy. No matter which type is selected, it must be financially sound and affordable.

Need for Disability and Long-term Care Insurance for Parents

A person's greatest asset is the ability to earn an income since that pays for housing, family needs, savings, education, retirement, and in the case of a family with a special needs member, that person's future.

Disability through illness or injury can threaten not only the parents' immediate financial well-being, but all of their development and future potential as well. It is absolutely essential that parents who are trying to plan for the care of a special needs child get disability insurance.

Disability insurance protects a person's income, and will help assure that appropriate funding is available to care for their child who is developmental disabled, as well as funding for the entire family.

Similarly, a family member's long-term care needs can quickly soak up funds dedicated to retirement or not already sequestered for the future care of a child with developmental disabilities. The average costs for private rooms in nursing homes can be very expensive, so check the costs in your state.

In October 2009, a MetLife survey titled the 2009 MetLife Market Survey of Nursing Home, Assisted Living, Adult Day Services, and Home Care Costs survey found that the average cost of a private room in a nursing home was $79,935/ $219 a day, increasing 3.3% from 2008, and in many areas, the cost is much higher. Read the full survey at www.MatureMarketInstitute.com

Resources for Parents of Those with Special Needs

Special Needs Trusts vary from state to state and can be very complicated to set up. The type of lawyer you need is an eldercare attorney, preferably one specializing in Special Needs Trusts. This is why when choosing a financial representative it is important to choose a person who focuses on special needs planning because he or she should be able to help you find the resources needed to help you formulate a plan.

Where Do I Begin?

- Speak to your local government agencies to find out what benefits your child is eligible for and the restrictions involved. If your child is in school, counselors there can point you in the right direction.

- If your child is in school, during his or her IEP, ask the teachers and psychologists what level of independence is projected for your child.

- Speak to a Financial Representative who focuses on special needs planning. There are many companies that work in this area, and some are:

  a. The Guardian Life Insurance Company (Forest Hills Financial Group is an agency for them)

  b. MetLife

  c. Mass Mutual

What qualities should your financial representative have?

- Your financial representative needs to make you feel comfortable. You must trust the person you will be working with and have faith in the financial stability of the company he or she represents.

- He or she needs to have contacts with eldercare attorneys. It is essential the attorney and financial representative work closely together.

- A helpful quality is the advisor's ability to empathize emotionally, which is essential in these situations.

- You want someone who not only takes a genuine interest in the well-being of the special needs person in your family, but the entire family as well.

When Should I Plan?

- The sooner you begin planning for your child the better. Envision your child having to rely on others and having no finances to ease the unique challenges that present themselves. Is that something you want to happen? Effectively planning for your child's financial support throughout his life will eliminate that possibility.

- Creating a secure financial future for your child will give you peace of mind

- It will help alleviate stress on the family as a whole.

- Most importantly, you will know that regardless what tomorrow brings, you can continue to be your child's greatest asset and know that the dreams you have for you or your child will be carried out, no matter what.

Planning Checklist

1. Talk to your family about your wishes, and inquire about theirs.

2. Speak to your child's doctor or teachers, with regard to his or her independence in the future.

3. Evaluate the needs of your entire family, not just the child who has a developmental disability.

4. Speak to a Financial Representative who focuses on special needs planning. She or he will be able help you evaluate the needs of your entire family, as well as find an attorney, and accountant.

5. Set up a Will, and a Living Will.

6. Make sure that your family, and caregivers are educated on the "fine print" of government benefits

7. Speak to an eldercare attorney, one who specializes in special needs.

About The Authors: Kim A. Schnepper, CLTC (Certified Long Term Care) specialist, and a Financial Representative, specializes in helping families who have children with developmental disabilities, as well as helping all families create proper plans for their future.

She and Martin Cherinn work with most financial companies, so they can best suit the needs of their clients. They focus on special needs planning, charitable giving, but most importantly they make sure that you, your child, and entire family receive the proper help and guidance needed.

Forest Hills Financial Group
122 East 42nd Street, Suite 2200
New York, NY 10168
Kim A. Schnepper, 212-687-8901 — kim_schnepper@fhfg.com
Martin Cherrin, 646-638-9853 — martin_cherrin@fhfg.com

Mr. Cherrin is a Registered Representative of Park Avenue Securities LLC (PAS), 95-25 Queens Blvd. 10th Floor, Rego Park, NY 11374. Securities products and services are offered through PAS, (718) 268-9255.

He and Ms. Schnepper are Financial Representatives of Guardian Life Insurance Company of America (Guardian), New York, NY. PAS is an indirect wholly owned subsidiary of Guardian. PAS is a member of FINRA, SIPC.

Forest Hills Financial Group is not a wholly owned subsidiary of the Guardian. The information presented here is designed for educational purposes and is not intended to be tax or legal advice. Guardian, its agents, subsidiaries and employees do not give tax or legal advice. For specific advice, seek and rely upon the advice of a qualified tax advisor or attorney.

The "Four Essentials"
To Securing Your Exceptional Child's Financial Future
John Dowson, Ch lp

Editor's Note: This section is for Canadian citizens only.

Benjamin Franklin first stated that the only two certainties in life are death and taxes. We all know we're going to die, but few of us like to ponder our mortality to any great degree, let alone the prospect of suddenly succumbing to a car accident or fatal illness.

For parents of exceptional children, who are already overloaded with daily responsibilities and concerns relating to their kids' needs, the preparations around a potential sudden death rarely factor in as a priority amid constant medical appointments, therapies, and professional consultations.

Planning for your child's future is not an easy thing to do, especially when you consider that you may not be around to see your plan come to fruition. Among the many questions parents ask when consulting with financial planners are:

What do our child's future caregivers need to know?

How much money should we leave?

How can we ensure that our child's inheritance will not affect his or her government benefits?

What type of lifestyle will he or she have after we're gone?

While the creation of Wills and family trusts are certainly recommended as foundations for securing your child's financial future, they comprise only part of the Life Plan that ought to be in place. While there is no cookie-cutter approach and every family's financial situation is unique, the following "Four Essentials" may help to guide you in preparing a comprehensive Life Plan for your exceptional son or daughter:

1. Educate Yourself about Available Financial Support and Services.

Prior to establishing a Life Plan, it is useful for parents to have a thorough knowledge of the financial support and services provided by their provincial government, and all of the federal income tax credits and deductions offered for people with disabilities.

2. Compile a List of Instructions for Future Caregivers.

In many ways, planning for your child's future is analogous to preparing to go away on a trip, except in the former case you're leaving with the knowledge that you're not going to return! Think back to a time when your child was young and you were planning to go out for the evening or away for the weekend.

What instructions did you give to the person who looked after your child? Chances are you informed the caregiver about your child's bedtime, the type of food he liked for his evening snack, how she liked to be tucked in, any medication he may have been taking and how it was to be administered, any special behaviors or needs that the caregiver ought to have been aware of, and whom to contact in case of an emergency.

In the same vein, it is necessary to compile a list of instructions for your child's future caregivers so that they will know how to care for your son or daughter according to his or her specific needs.

3. Determine a Budget.

It is also imperative that parents determine a budget around the financial costs of their child's lifetime needs and future lifestyle, conduct an estate inventory, and decide which financial resources they intend to employ in order to fund those needs.

4. Put Your Plan into Action.

Parents will also benefit from creating an up-to-date Will and appointing trustees for their child's trust, as well as a Special Needs Trust (or Absolute Discretionary, Henson type trust agreement) for their child's assets or inheritance. Most importantly, parents should compose a letter of intent in which they outline the following:

The trust's specific purpose.

How funds should be spent.

Procedures around opening a trust bank account and management of the trust.

Filing a trust income tax return.

Information around the use of the "preferred beneficiary election" (a tax-saving method for trusts to be explained in a future article).

Life Plan Essential #1:

Educate Yourself about Available Financial Support and Services.

Federal Credits and Deductions Offered for People with Special Needs.

According to the Government of Canada's Office of Disability Issues[1], more than 3 million Canadians have a disability and depend on someone for support. The definition of a caregiver according to the federal government is anyone who supports a person who is dependent on the taxpayer by reason of mental or physical infirmity.

While all caregivers are eligible to file or back file for the Disability Tax Credit (DTC), many people are unaware of its existence. The DTC is a non-refundable tax credit that reduces the amount of federal income tax payable and may even generate a refund for past taxation years.

1   Government of Canada Office of Disability Issues (ODI),"Canadian Disability Statistics, 2005" http://www.sdc.gc.ca/en/gateways/nav/top_nav/program/odi.shtml

Parents and caregivers of people with a disability can claim past income tax credits for up to ten years. Accordingly, people with disabilities and their caregivers can have their income tax returns reassessed back to 1996. People with disabilities or their caregivers who have never claimed the Disability Tax Credit (DTC) should claim it now!

Thousands of Canadian families who care for a person with a disability may be eligible to receive thousands of dollars in refunds from income tax they have already paid. Some claimants have received refunds of between $12,000 and $21,000 or more.

Benefits

Caregivers of individuals aged 18 and over, or people who have severe and prolonged cognitive or physical disabilities, are eligible to transfer the DTC to their tax return. If at anytime in the year the caregiver maintained a residence where their dependent lived, the caregiver may also be able to claim the Caregiver amount on their tax return and back file this up to ten years.

Parents who care for a child with a disability under age 18 may claim a reduced Disability Tax Credit (DTC). Families with low or modest incomes may also be eligible to receive the Child Disability Benefit.

Other Benefits of the DTC

Qualifying for the DTC is the yardstick which allows the individual or their caregiver to make a number of claims for medical expenses and deductions; such as education and tuition fees, attendant care, private nursing, daily-living aids, dental bills, prescription drugs, hearing aids, the adaptation of vehicles, travel expenses for medical treatment not locally available, therapy, group-home fees, talking books, tutoring, renovations, and to qualify as the beneficiary of a Registered Disability Savings Plan.

Finally, while federal tax legislation is applicable throughout Canada, each province and territory has its own financial supports and assets limits for people with disabilities. For more information on the specific social benefits legislation concerning financial support applicable to your province, visit your government website.

John Dowson, Ch lp, is the Executive Director of LifeTRUST Planning, a national company that serves exceptional families across the country. Visit his website for more information at www.life-trust.com

Chapter 16

Medical, Dental, and Other Health Issues

Chapter 16
Medical, Dental, and Other Health Issues

Bill Davis and Kumar Ramlall, M.D.

Finding the Right Physician, Bill's Story

people with autism succeed in life through their strengths

—Dr. Stephen Shore

At age five, my son, Chris did not speak. His pediatrician asked us to wait awhile, and said he would talk. Chris spoke when he was six.

As parents, we are naturally impatient, and want answers now. Of course, we want those answers to be right. Doctors see a certain set symptoms, which can represent any number of things, from a child with neurological problems, a developmentally delayed child, or a child with autism. You need to know that it's not always a cut and dry situation, so be patient as you find the best Pediatrician for your child.

Most children's hospitals have several types of specialists on staff, so this is a good way for you to find a doctor who specializes in any problems your child may have. If you suspect your child has autism, talk to other parents of disabled children, visit a children's hospital, or ask your doctor to recommend a physician familiar with autism. Some of the types of doctors and specialists you will find at children's hospitals are clinical psychologists, speech and language pathologists, social workers, occupational therapists, developmental pediatricians, neurologists and more.

We received our diagnosis from an involved and informed team at The Kennedy Krieger Institute. Dr. Rebecca Landa led a group of dedicated therapists, devoted to children with autism. We credit our team for the progress Chris made when he was young, and the earlier you identify autism,

170

the sooner you can implement interventions.

If your child has autism, one type of doctor who provides bio-medical (application of natural sciences to medicine) interventions, such as diet and supplementation is called a DAN (Defeat Autism Now) doctor. You can find these doctors and get more information about their therapies at www.autism.com

A good resource for you is Dr. William Shaw's, *Biological Treatments for Autism and Pervasive Development Disorder* (PDD) and the sequel, *Autism: Beyond The Basics*. These are incredibly complete guides to bio-medical interventions.

Dental Care is Essential

At one point, I was doing so many other things with Chris, I nearly forgot about dental care. I cannot begin to tell you how many dental surgeries and emergency visits Chris has had.

Good dental hygiene is so important. Start early to find dentists who will take your child's sensory issues into consideration and do things like dim the lights and minimize noise. Proper care and frequent examinations can prevent yet another obstacle your child may have to endure.

Practice behavior at the dentist with social stories and scripting. Bring toys that will comfort your child. Let him know, step by step, what will take place. Rehearse, "Open," "Hands down," and especially, "No biting."

A Father and a Doctor
Kumar Ramlall, M.D.

While I am a physician, current Chair of the National Examination Board in his specialty, and nationally acknowledged clinical teacher, I am writing this section as both a doctor and a parent.

I want you to know that you have a right to make a guilt-free choice about how your child's treatment proceeds and whether or not you choose to use medications. Over the years, I have seen too many loving parents make NO choice, and never see their child's full potential because they could not commit to a course of therapy. I believe this is due to guilt, often brought on by well-meaning family and friends.

171

I know how any parent feels, firsthand, because my own was diagnosed with ASD. I know what it is like to be unable to hug your child because he cannot tolerate your touch or even feed your child because all the food seems to hurt. I also know what it is like to implement all the regular medical protocols and yet still see your child suffer.

It is easy for me to hold two views – one, traditional medicine, and the other, a more complimentary approach. These seem to combine the best of both worlds, and may offer more choices to your child. The reason is because ASD is a problem of the brain, and with our advances in neuroplasticity, we now know the brain can repair itself.

Children who have autism, might have problems with swallowing and speech, but it is primarily their brain, and not their mouth, that has the problem. They might have problems breathing, but it is not their lungs causing the problem. They may have problems walking, but it is not their legs that have the problem.

With the brain issue firmly established, I vigorously defend a parent's right to choose to help his child with or without the use of medications.

My son is a success story for parents who choose to help their children without medication. He is on a program of therapy where one of the first markers of success was weaning him off "brain medication." We worked long and hard to accomplish this. My son has achieved this, and he has gone from the third "worst" of 10,000 children on psychological testing done at about three years of age, to a child of seven who is reading and applying university-level material in various subjects. He has attended and summarized five day-long business courses; is tremendously physically fit; speaks and conducts himself very maturely, and writes in an even more sophisticated manner.

Most of all, he is loved and adored by his profoundly grateful parents. Coming off medications, pursuing our daily program, and taking the measures we've used to help our son have enormous self-esteem, have all helped.

This said, I definitely believe there is a role for brain medications. They can support life, so people can thrive with the brains they have. We would not deny children with heart problems the medications they need, so why deny brain medications if needed?

Children with brain problems deserve the chance to have their problems "fixed" the same as children with heart problems. They want to be loved just like other children, they deserve to live life to its fullest without disabilities or limitations.

There is a balanced place for medications alongside other traditional and complimentary treatments. We should resolve to accept and be grateful for the improvements we see in our children and to keep an open mind about the use of medications and alternative treatments.

There will always be someone, who criticizes our decisions as a parent, no matter what we choose. Do not ever forget that you, the mother or father, has the right and the duty to do what you judge best for your child.

About the Author: Dr. Kumar Ramlall, BSc, MD, FAAP, FRCPC, FCCP, is a Clinical Associate Professor at the University of Alberta specializing in Pediatric Pulmonology, and is the Chief Examiner of the Royal College Pediatric Respirology Board. His medical practice previously focused on children with the most complex medical problems, helping them get the most "function" and the most "living" with the medical conditions they had. His son has Autism Spectrum Disorder and is now showing marked improvement. He and his wife are experts at using principles from business and personal development to improve the outcomes for pre-school children with developmental problems and are committed to teaching other families these skills. Go to www.ThinkTAction.com to get more information about using these methods for your child.

Chapter 17

Fitness for Special Students

Chapter 17
Fitness for Special Students

Eric Chessen

Fitness for Optimal Futures

Fitness is a gateway to important life skills like reading, writing and communication...
—Pat Wyman, M.A.

In the U.S., those educational and life skill goals considered important in the mainstream will undergo a modified or "adapted" process in special education. This seems a natural and logical process. After all, the goal of the special education classroom is to provide students with an optimized learning environment which allows them an eventual path into mainstream society. Unfortunately, the failings of the general education system are evident in special education. Physical fitness is the most apparent example.

A Brief History of What Went Wrong

Several decades ago, physical education for the general youth population focused on developing basic foundations of movement, coordination, strength, and cardiovascular functioning. Calisthenics and gymnastics (jumping jacks, push-ups, and squat thrusts, among many other exercises) were central to the curriculum, and the foundations of general fitness were established prior to specialization in more advanced athletic pursuits. Over the past three decades, general fitness in physical education has fallen wayside to sports-based programs.

The problem with sports-based physical education is that it is completely backwards from a developmental standpoint. That whole crawling, walking, running thing works in a particular order for a reason. If a teacher took a class of first grade students and decided, on the very first day of math, to begin teaching calculus, there would not be a high success rate. In fact, all of the students would probably fail, become quite frustrated and discouraged.

The big misconception about fitness and sports exists among both parents and educators. Participating in sports does not equal physical fitness. Sports are a highly specialized area of physical fitness. As illustrated in the math class example, a general foundation must be developed in order to ensure mastery of more complex constructs. Sports are branches, physical fitness is the roots and trunk.

Individuals on the autism spectrum often lack the initiative to engage in novel play or attempt new movements or activities. In fact, several research studies have demonstrated a marked difference between the gross motor function abilities of children and adolescents with autism and 'neurotypical' peers. Individuals with autism often exhibit deficits in gross motor function and physical ability. They do not take the initiative to run, jump, hop, climb, or tumble. Given that most 'neurotypical' children are now sedentary and the playgrounds are empty, the vast differences in physical ability are becoming less obvious. This is a scary proposition on all fronts.

Consider the combination of the problems discussed thus far. We have a cultural and educational climate that is not conducive to physical health and wellness and, when PE actually does exist, it focuses primarily upon introducing sports. This is not a diatribe against sports; rather it is illustrating the design flaws in a sports-first PE curriculum and culture. Those children and adolescents who gravitate towards and succeed in sports in order to get exercise, and those young people who do not play sports well are often just not the 'active type' And that's okay!

Why Being Inactive Is Absolutely, Positively, NOT Okay

Exercise is a gateway towards optimization in all areas of development. From physical well-being, to self-regulation, self-esteem, self-efficacy, and socialization, all open up new possibilities for future vocations, and being able to succeed in daily life challenges. Being able to pick up something heavy, safely and efficiently, is one of the greatest gifts you can give somebody. It is a gift of self-sufficiency and independence. The point of physical fitness as a curriculum, whether in school or at home, is to develop movement patterns and physical skills that are present and accessible beyond the exercise session.

The key to a successful school or home-based exercise program is to develop skills that can be generalized to other situations. If an individual on the autism spectrum is able to perform a proper squat to pick up a ball, fantastic. However, the real proof lies in their ability to perform that same movement when picking up another object in a non-exercise situation. This is where we begin to realize how important physical fitness is for life skills.

While not all children may gravitate towards sports, exercise is a necessary part of optimal development for all individuals. Adolescent males, who are undergoing regular hormonal tidal waves, require vigorous activity to strengthen muscles elongated by growth spurts. With all the evidence supporting the benefits of exercise for emotional well-being and self-esteem, it is practically criminal not to provide a physical outlet for adolescents and teens.

Many of the older athletes with whom I have worked spend much of their waking time sitting, watching television, or "disengaging" in other sedentary activities. It is not a stretch to suggest that these individuals are hypo-stimulated, and do not receive an adequate, or healthy, amount of physical stimuli. Stereotypical activities, including hand flapping, jumping up and down, and preservative tactile stimulation via rubbing against materials or objects, can be signs of hypo or restricted physical stimulation. We have bodies, and those bodies are designed to move regardless of our ability or desire to play sports. Every individual deserves the opportunity not only to move correctly, but also to engage in vigorous physical activity on a regular basis.

Stereotypy provides the neuromuscular and central nervous systems (CNS) with input. A lack of environmental outlets can create a need for self-stimulation. Engaging in physical activity can greatly reduce these systemic deficits. Educators and parents often report that individuals with autism have difficulty concentrating or remaining task oriented. They may wander from an activity, engage in stereotypical behaviors, or have other self-regulatory problems. The introduction of physical movement can aid in developing self-regulatory skills. Vigorous physical activity performed in short intervals throughout the day can provide the central nervous system, plus muscular, and neuromuscular systems, with an abundance of beneficial stimulation.

Over the past two decades, there has been much scientific and public discussion about the importance of the mind-body "connection." Rather than a connection, the brain and muscular anatomy share an intricate network of neurons. Essentially, rather than the brain and muscular systems being exclusive with some wires stringing them together, there is an intimate and fascinating interaction occurring at all times. With regard to education, particular emphasis is placed on the cognitive aspect of development, while there is far less planning and training for physical skills. Proper physical education not only aids in the acquisition of physical abilities, but in cognitive and emotional capacities as well.

What Is Authentic Physical Fitness?

Physical fitness is our ability to meet daily challenges and to tap into our potential to reach new goals and challenges. Physical fitness is a general adaptation process, meaning that the skills should be applicable to a variety of activities, including both life and play skills.

Again, using the example of mathematics, suppose we are teaching addition, and a student provides the answer "5" to the equation "2+2 = ____." The answer "5" is obviously incorrect, though quite close to the correct response.

Still, we would not validate the incorrect answer as acceptable, yet we do validate movement deficits as normal or fine. Simply because the body can perform a movement does not equal the movement being performed correctly. Now it must be pointed out that there is a far wider variability for movement than for math. As individuals, we all move slightly differently in accordance with our physical form and history of movement. Some knees will turn out more during squatting, or hip-flexion movements, some individuals have abnormally great range of motion in their shoulders. It is important to remember that individual movement patterns can and do vary, and equally important to recognize when there are deficits and pronounced compensations.

Fitness is, when potential is fully actualized, establishing a joy of movement and instilling a desire to work and play. Fitness is having an abundance of energy and the ability to self-regulate. Fitness should be contagious, a social activity that inspires friendship, camaraderie, and goal-orientation. Fitness requires patience, self-determination, focus, and a sense of purpose.

The Importance of Family Fitness

Parents, siblings, and family members need to be active participants in order for a fitness program to become a fitness lifestyle. One of my greatest challenges as a fitness specialist and consultant is to phase out a parents' reliance on a professional and begin implementing programs with their child. A twelve-year-old individual with autism may gain some benefit from a fitness session performed for 45 minutes each week working with a professional, but the benefits of a single exercise session do not negate sedentary lifestyle, stresses, and a poor diet the rest of the week. If parents and family members are active and engage in fitness lifestyles, it is far more conducive to a child developing healthy habits and having access to fitness modalities

Parents will make great sacrifices for their children, financially, socially, and physically. Choices are often made despite detriment to a parent in one of these three categories. The question must be posed however: Who will take care of *you*? Being active and healthy yourself, as a parent, is one of the greatest opportunities you can provide a child with autism. Having energy, enthusiasm, and the general well-being that accompany a fitness lifestyle are huge factors in long-term goal planning and the overall success of a family and its individual members. Fitness for parents does not have to differ much from fitness programs for children with special needs. An eventual goal of performing exercise (primarily resistance and mobility) 20-30 minutes 4-5 times a week will yield tremendous benefits, and will certainly aid in the development of a fitness lifestyle. You don't even have to pick up a pair of leg warmers or matching sweatbands.

The Abridged Exercise Encyclopedia

- Squatting/Bending
- Pushing
- Pulling
- Rotation
- Locomotion

Squatting /bending and straightening of the legs. Squatting is a natural movement that we are absolutely, positively supposed to be doing. Squatting exercises can include bending the knees deep to grab a ball, lunging forward or laterally, crawls, and hops. More advanced movements include skipping, jumping, and running.

Pushing movements require stabilization of the trunk and the ability to "root" into the ground. Many daily life activities require pushing movements, from opening a door to putting away boxes on a shelf. Pushing is a relatively simple premise, though I frequently work with young individuals on the spectrum that have difficulty planting their feet and using the upper body for movement while the lower body provides stability.

Medicine ball (referred to as a med ball or exercise ball) chest passes, sandbag or SandBell™, overhead presses, and various other throws or movements away from the body with weighted objects can provide great foundations for pushing.

Pulling should be practiced as much as pushing. Pulling movements can be performed with some of the same equipment as pushing movements. A light medicine ball can be pulled off the floor (also incorporating proper squatting movement); a resistance band can be pulled while the feet are anchored to the floor.

Rotation is possibly the most ignored movement pattern. We rotate when getting in and out of a car. We rotate when we have to catch a ball. We rotate when reaching for the soap in the shower. Rotation is a secondary motion in many athletic pursuits as well. Poor rotation can also lead to neck and lower back injuries and impingements. I prefer to use lightly weighted (2-6 lb.) medicine balls to teach rotation. Careful not to over-rotate! A little bit of turn is enough.

Locomotion, or our ability to get from one point to another on our feet (usually), is often the most obvious deficit in children with Autism Spectrum Disorder (ASD). Gait patterning can be challenging. Many of the exercises mentioned above will have beneficial effects on the gait cycle, due to the increased mobility of the muscle groups as well as the newly developing strength, postural integrity, and focus.

Chapter 18

Health and Nutritional Needs

Chapter 18

Health and Nutritional Needs

Julie Matthews

Diet and Autism, What You Need To Know

Parents are quickly learning that food choices can help their sons and daughters become healthier and reach their full potential. In addition to traditional behavioral therapy and other pharmaceutical treatments, pediatricians, researchers, and nutritionists increasingly recommend that parents implement autism diets, autism-specific nutrition, and specialized supplementation. Even television's respected Dr. Oz recently said, "Some of the most promising treatments for autism come from changing your child's diet."

Our children's tomorrow lies in their health today...

—Eric Chessen

Ultimately, we know that one major road to autism recovery begins with diet. Try adding and removing foods to improve your child's health. Notably, gluten and casein seem to be problematic for the children with autism, so, with your doctor's advice, try to avoid them. Gluten and casein are protein fractions. Gluten is in all wheat, barley, rye and most oat products. Casein is in all dairy products.

By adding an autism diet, supplementation, enzymes and consistently healthy nutrition to your autism pediatrician's treatment plan, your child has the opportunity to have better sleep, higher cognitive ability, less pain, fewer rashes, a positive change in digestion, and improvement in various behaviors.

When you correctly and diligently implement an autism diet, most parents

184

and pediatricians report improvement in gastrointestinal problems, diarrhea, constipation, language, learning, focus, attention, eye contact, behavior, sleep difficulties, toilet training, skin rashes/eczema and body pain.

There are a number of autism diets you may want to research. They include the Gluten-Free Casein-Free (GFCF) Diet, Specific Carbohydrate Diet (SCD), Gut and Psychology Syndrome (GAPS) Diet, Low Oxalate Diet, Body Ecology Diet, Feingold Diet and the Weston A. Price Diet.

Most parents begin with the GFCF Diet because it seems to work more quickly and is easy to implement.

When we identify autism as a whole body disorder, it's easy to understand what happens inside your child's body, cells, and brain, and how food affects the whole body and its biochemistry.

Poor digestion can lead to a condition known as leaky gut, which is poor absorption of nutrients, inflammatory responses to foods that are not broken down, and a burden to the detoxification system. Nutrients are essential to all biochemical and brain function. Adequate nutritional statuses require the consumption of nutrient dense food and proper digestion to break down and absorb those foods.

Additionally, your child's response to foods such as gluten and casein can create an opiate or inflammatory reaction that can affect the brain, causing foggy thinking, affecting attention, language, and learning.

It is important to understand just how critical the gut's role is in autism symptoms. The gut breaks down your child's food so they can have the nutrients needed to support biochemistry and allow the brain to function properly. The largest part of the immune system (70%) is found in the gut, and that system is often imbalanced in autism causing an inability to fight viruses, yeast, and other pathogens properly while contributing an overactive inflammatory and allergic response. Toxins in the gut often affect the brain, and 90% of the brain's, feel-good chemical, serotonin, is in the gut.

How Diet Can Help with Autism

By supporting digestion and biochemistry through diet, you most likely will be able to improve autism symptoms. Here are several examples of how good food and nutrients can improve the health of the gut, the whole body's biochemistry, and positively affect the conditions and symptoms of autism.

Nutrient Deficiencies: Doctors say that nutrient deficiencies are common among children with autism. In addition to getting a wide variety of nutrients through foods, supporting digestion is important. Your doctor will want to help show you how to:

- Increase the quality and digestibility of food.
- Sneak in vegetables for picky eaters.
- Juice vegetables and consume homemade bone broths.
- Add supplementation, as recommended, and medications as prescribed.

Leaky Gut and Gut Inflammation: Improving digestion, reducing inflammation, and healing the gut are important steps in overall health and healing.

- Remove foods that inflame the gut such as gluten, casein, and soy.
- Add foods that heal the gut and are anti-inflammatory such as antioxidant and probiotic-rich foods, such as non-dairy yogurt and raw sauerkraut.
- Add foods that support beneficial bacteria growth (probiotics).

Yeast Overgrowth: Yeast is a harmful organism that can affect energy level, clarity of thought, and intestinal health. Yeast overgrowth is often triggered by heavy antibiotic use, common in children with autism with poor bacteria-fighting ability. Yeast overgrowth creates gut inflammation and decreases gut function.

- Remove sugars.
- Remove foods containing yeast.
- Reduce refined starches and, in some cases, remove them.
- Add probiotic-rich foods, such as dairy, or non-dairy probiotic capsules if your doctor says that's the best plan for your child.

Toxicity and Poor Detoxification: When children's detoxification systems are not working optimally or are overburdened by preexisting toxins, avoiding additional toxins from food is important. Some food-based chemicals can cross the blood-brain barrier and affect the brain, possibly creating hyperactivity, aggression, irritability, and self-injurious behavior. For optimal health, most nutritionists will tell you to have your child:

- Avoid food additives.
- Avoid toxins in food supply and during meal preparation.

- Eat organically.
- Add foods that support the liver.

Poor Methylation and Sulfation Biochemistry: Methylation, transsulfuration, and sulfation are just one set of biochemical pathways that do not function optimally for many children with autism. These pathways can be supported by avoiding certain substances that are processed, and adding certain items that enhance the pathways. For those with decreased methylation and sulfation, many nutritionists recommend:

- Removing phenolic foods, such as artificial ingredients, and foods high in natural salicylates, amines and glutamates, such as grapes, raisins, apples, berries, almonds, honey and more…

- Improving methylation and sulfation through supplementation, following your doctor's advice. This may include such things as Vitamin B12, folate, B6, DMG/TMG, magnesium and zinc supplements.

I hope that you can see the possibilities for positive influence and realize that diet can help your child's autism. Diet is a powerful personal tool; it has few downsides and is accessible to everyone. With diet, parents have great control over choices that can have immediate positive impact in the health of children.

The most successful parents and children in my private practice are those that take steps to carefully implement autism diets. They believe in healing, that recovery is possible, and that through calculated food choices they can make a difference. While modern medical channels present few options, parents are following Hippocrates' traditional advice of letting food be thy medicine.

The easiest and most important initial action, no matter what diet you choose, is to remove artificial ingredients and junk food. Artificial ingredients are highly toxic and very difficult for the liver to break down - they are associated with hyperactivity, asthma, aggression, irritability, and sleep disturbances. Once you realize the harmful nature of certain foods, you'll naturally choose *not* to include them, or "eliminate" them, from your child's diet.

Food additives and ingredients to avoid:

- Artificial colors: red #40, yellow #5.
- Artificial flavors: vanillin.
- Preservatives: BHA, BHT, TBHQ.
- Monosodium glutamate: MSG, hydrolyzed vegetable protein and other hydrolyzed items, autolyzed yeast or yeast extract.
- Artificial sweeteners.
- Trans fats, partially hydrogenated oil found in many commercial products such as mayonnaise, margarine, peanut butter products, fast foods, fried food, and baked goods.

The most important dietary principle is to *start*. It sounds simple but start somewhere. Begin with a simple diet change such as getting rid of all artificial ingredients and see what's next.

I know what you are thinking, "My child is picky and very inflexible with eating new foods. I'm never going to be able to get him to eat anything other than wheat and dairy, and never mind anything "healthy." I also understand that you are really wondering if an autism diet will help your child and their symptoms.

I appreciate these concerns. I have had some very picky eaters in my nutrition practice. Many children ate only bread and dairy, others subsisted on just pancakes and fries. However, there are solid reasons why these children are so one-sided in their food choices, primarily cravings.

When a person's body creates opiates from foods, it's easy to feel addicted and crave nothing but those foods. If a yeast overgrowth is present, people generally want to eat carbohydrates or sugars only. Children eventually narrow their food choices to include *only* those that make them "feel better" (in the short term). It's worth trying to diet because once the child is past the cravings (a few days to a few weeks), they often expand food choices dramatically and it becomes much easier to do.

More children, as well as their sleep-deprived parents, are recovering with an autism diet.

I encourage every parent who has a child with autism to try diet, read, and learn more. I, like you, am committed to helping children with autism get better. Nourishing hope comes from the depths of our hearts and is fueled by love and devotion. Always have hope.

About the Author: Julie Matthews is an internationally respected autism nutrition specialist and author of the award-winning book, *"Nourishing Hope for Autism,"* and the creator of *"Cooking to Heal: Autism Nutrition and Cooking Class"* (DVD). Julie provides diet and nutrition intervention guidance backed by scientific research and applied clinical experience. She presents at the leading biomedical autism conferences in the US and abroad. Visit www.nourishinghope.com.

Julie Matthews is not a physician. She does not diagnose or treat disease. This article is not intended to replace a one-on-one relationship with a qualified health-care professional, and is not intended to provide medical advice. For medical advice, always seek a physician. This article is solely intended as a sharing of knowledge and information based upon the experience and research of the author.

Chapter 19

Attending a University or Community College

Chapter 19

Attending a University or Community College

Bill Davis and Dr. Stephen Shore

...in the next human rights movement we will shatter myths and tear down walls...

—William Stillman

University, Colleges, Community Colleges

We've written this chapter to speak to you, the parent, and additionally, to speak directly to your college or college bound student. You may want to print various sections that are the most helpful for you and your child.

When your child with autism is researching universities, colleges or community colleges, look for a small, quiet campus, with plenty of trees and pleasant restful areas. People will suggest that this is a great time for your child to socialize, but don't pressure your child into socializing.

You may want to print this list for yourself and your child, because these are the things facing your child as he or she attends college. Deal with them ahead of time, and you will see a happier, more comfortable, successful child.

Notes For Parents. Your Child Will:

- face deadlines, new regulations, financial aid (in some cases), cancelled classes, and room changes

- navigate from hall to hall, quickly and efficiently

- know specific locations to take private breaks. For example, restrooms are wonderful places to flap. There are some children who need to self-stimulate, so help your child understand that waving your hands furiously in psychology 101 is probably not the best place.

- need to know how to acknowledge feeling overloaded and when it is best to take a break

- need to know that the college classroom is not like playing a movie. There is no rewind or pause button for the professor, and if your child misses too many classes, it may be hard to catch up.

- realize just how many distractions there will be during a lecture; the kinds of noise, the type of lighting, and how it will feel when students enter and leave the room

- need to know how to locate a counselor and a support system on the campus

Notes To College Bound Students:

- Reach out and connect with other people with autism.

- Find autistic self-advocates who will suggest coping strategies.

- Familiarize yourself with the campus.

- Obtain a map of the campus or draw one you like.

- Stroll through the buildings slowly.

- Determine the times when there is a huge rush of student traffic, and try to avoid it.

- Make sure you have access to a laptop computer of your own. Not only will you be working, writing, and studying with it, but, you will be able to keep your finger on the rapid pulse of college life.

- Contact an advisor and schedule weekly meetings. Colleges always have support references, so keep them in a favorite place, where you can locate them quickly.

- Talk to housing and let them know about any sensory issues you might have.

- Call food services if you are following a special diet, and if possible, make sure you have some of your own, specialized food in your room, if it is not perishable. Some colleges and universities have dorm rooms with refrigerators. If possible, get one.

Remember, there is no shame in seeking assistance. Perhaps you can find a supportive mentor who is older and been attending the college longer. You want to live as independently as possible. You need to pay bills, do laundry, keep your room clean, budget yourself, and learn cooperative living.

You don't always have to live away from home. Try an online university or take a few credits at a local community college. Once again, take it slow, get used to new experiences and different ways of coexisting. College life is structured, but not in the ways you may already know. You have a lot of free time, and have to set up your own study schedule. Study areas can give you a quiet place to concentrate on your work. You can have a tutor or tutors if you need them. Once you are settled and confident, look for a recreational activity that interests you. Some people like bowling leagues, discussion groups, or taking trips. The options are limitless, so make certain you really like the recreational activity you choose.

The school will provide counselor to help you manage stress. Learning new social skills will be challenging. Observe others. Practice will help you make the leap into college life. Rehearse, practice, and request help. You may not want to disclose your disorder, but revealing aversions, allergies, and social issues is a wise thing to do. You will notice that people will respond with much more understanding and kindness, if they know more about you, what helps comfort you, and which things make you uncomfortable.

Acquiring knowledge and finding a career path are priorities, but you will also come face to face with "small talk," dating, parties, and dorm life. Ask for advice, and find a friend to trust and confide in. Stay strong, trust your spirituality and remember that being different is beautiful! Teasing and bullying exist on the university level because bullies never grow up. Work hard, make strong connections, and pursue a quality education.

Always, always capitalize on your strengths. Earn your diploma and live life to the fullest.

Temple Grandin's HBO special, called "Temple Grandin," may be something you want to watch before attending college. This is a real life story of a woman with autism who faced many challenges, thriving despite all of them.

Parent Tip: Even at college, your child may experience bullying or cruelty. Help your child prepare, listen to your child, and ensure a support system is in place on campus.

Adjusting to Life on Campus

If you are college bound, or in college already, there is no shame in seeking accommodations (changes in schedules or testing, or living arrangements that help you cope with your autism), so use them to your advantage. There are laws in place to support you. Locate disability services on campus and in town. Have your doctor or therapist recommend and contact a physician knowledgeable about autism, close to the college of your choice. Chat with your professors about your strengths and needs. You may even want to write a letter to your professors, telling them more about you and your needs. You may need to sit in the same seat daily or get permission to take a number of breaks. This letter may help you more than you realize.

If you have a hard time with social interaction, don't let it get you down. You have not failed, so do not feel depressed. In order to survive, you will need to acquire the ability to detect non-verbal cues, and read facial expressions.

Ask yourself the following questions and create appropriate responses by seeking guidance:

Do I sometimes misunderstand or avoid people?

Do I defer pain or just avoid dealing with it?

Do I recall times when I was so confused I just stopped listening?

How many times have I been so involved in a project that I have forgotten to eat or relieve myself?

Stephen Shore, who has Asperger's, and truly understands you, writes a section right after these notes to you and your parents, so you'll want to read it.

- Do not limit yourself. Start planning for college in high school. Talk to your guidance counselor. Approaches and supports need to be individualized. Select college courses that complement your career choices.

- Find students with similar interests. Pursue activities that are enjoyable and soothing. There are many opportunities on campus to volunteer.

- Dorm living might put a strain on your ability to adjust. Request a private room or arrange for off-campus living arrangements. Disclose any medical conditions, such as allergies, to teachers, advisors and other students so they can help you if needed.

- Be aware that your rituals and coping mechanisms can make you seem like an easy person to bully. Ask your counselor how to deal with bullies. We understand that seeking normalcy can backfire, so make every effort not to feel ostracized. It is only when you give people permission, that they can make you feel badly about yourself. Don't give them that kind of power over you.

- You must recognize and at times indulge your special needs. Request more study time or longer exam periods. Take semesters off and don't carry a heavy course load.

- Exercise will keep you fit, and is a good social outlet. Going to the gym may be your downtime, although you may want to go at off-hours, so it is quieter. Be sure and read Eric Chessen's chapter on fitness in the book, before heading off to college.

- Hygiene and personal appearance are important, so make the effort.

- Talk to your resident assistant. Let him know of any problems or needs you might have.

The academic part of college is not usually a problem for you. It is the other things, like social activities and noise that may cause challenges. Colleges are well aware of the influx of students with autism. They have added classes and programming to help students cope and adjust. The Organization for Autism Research has produced videos to educate college staffs about autism.

Achieving in Higher Education with Autism/Developmental Disabilities (AHEADD) at www.aheadd.org helps college students on the spectrum. They provide courses on acclimation to campus life.

Autism awareness is alive and kicking! Resources, parents, friends and support systems are available. Accept their help and strive for excellence!

Be a success story

Here's a quick story for you about Stephen Shore that you may enjoy.

Kate, Chris, and I went to Canada to present at one of Karen's conferences. Neither Kate nor Chris had met Stephen Shore before. We checked into our hotel, and began to stroll around, when we noticed a very large indoor water park. It was complete with waves, waterfalls, swimming and Chris' favorite, the hot tub.

We notice a bearded man, standing alone, under the cascading stream of water, flapping. Kate looked up at me and said, "I guess that's Stephen!" Stephen Shore has become an icon and an invaluable resource in the world of autism. I am so thankful that he wrote the following section for you, and I am honored to know him.

College for People on the Autism Spectrum
By Stephen Shore, Professor and man with Asperger's

We have noticed an increased prevalence of autism since the late 1980's. Some people surmise the increase is due to greater awareness, a broadening of the definition of autism, and better diagnostics. For example, according to the Annual Report to Congress on Special Education, the numbers of children diagnosed with mental retardation continues to fall over time whereas those identified with other learning disabilities, including autism has risen. While this is an interesting thought, one is hard pressed to consider why this "exchange" of diagnoses is responsible for the rise in numbers of people on the autism spectrum.

Others look towards environmental toxins, the possible role of vaccines, and other biomedical etiologies to explain the increased numbers. Definitive answers to this question remain elusive, but the truth is likely to involve a combination of a number of causes, some yet to be identified.

What we do know is that significant number of young adults who are on the leading edge of this increased prevalence rate, are beginning to make their way into colleges and universities. Therefore, greater understanding of autism in teenagers and young adults will help immeasurably, in promoting success at the higher education level.

Transition Preparation

Ever since middle school, when I knew what going to college was about, I sensed that it would be the right place for me to be. During high school, I visited my older sister a number of times while she was in college. Each time I visited, I felt happy and satisfied. Although I didn't know it then, I was preparing for my transition to university life. In my senior year of high school, I applied to, and got accepted into the same university my sister attended. I even signed up to stay in the same dorm complex she lived in during her college years. By the time I arrived, my sister had graduated, but she lived nearby the campus. As I described earlier, my transition work, between high school and college was finished by the time I got to college.

If you can find a way to familiarize yourself with university life, while you are still in high school, it will smooth the transition towards the college experiences. Some of you may be able to handle the traditional "live away from home, while attending school full time," type of life, while others may need to tackle the entire college experience in separate components, one at a time.

For example, you may want to live at home and take just one or two classes at a nearby college at first. It's also important to realize that it's possible that you may just not be ready for a college experience at one particular time, and may wish to pursue a higher education over a longer period of time.

Attending the University

University life was a utopia for me. Bullying vanished, as my fellow students were more interested in whom the other person was, rather than how much they were like someone else. Courses were interesting and there was enough diversity within the 25,000 students, that it was easy to find like-minded people. If I wanted to ride my bicycle at midnight, I could find someone just as odd to go with me!

Like others on the autism spectrum, I craved the grade school structure that university life provided with days, weeks, semesters, and academic year. However, it is important to be aware of a significant difference is that with this structure, you will have to be much more self-directed. Your parents are not there to make sure you wake up on time to get to an early class. No one insists you eat decent meals, tells you to do your homework, structures your time, or lets you know it is time to go to sleep. Fortunately, these things were not much of a challenge for me, and I got through my undergraduate degrees in music education, alongside a program in accounting and information systems, all with university honors.

My friend, Eric Chessen, who wrote the fitness chapter in this book, says, "It is challenging enough living in a world that is just beginning to understand people with autism, so when you attend and graduate from college, the real honor is letting some others with autism know they can follow that same path.

Years ago, we didn't know much about autism. Few believed that anyone on the autism spectrum could make it through college. For example, when I told my music education advisor that my diagnosis of autism was creating challenges in my passing a doctoral qualifier exam, he boomed out, "Gee…I didn't know you were autistic." Perhaps now he serves as a sort of ambassador when he discusses an "interesting meeting with a doctoral student" with his colleagues. I am glad to report that his department has a much greater awareness of and gives more support to students with various learning challenges. This is why it is so important for a student with autism to have sufficient awareness of their own learning style, in order to self-advocate for their educational needs.

In my books, *Understanding Autism for Dummies*, and *Ask and Tell: Self-Advocacy and Disclosure for People on the Autism Spectrum*, I discuss a number of ways of involving students in their own educational plans to the greatest extent of their abilities. This is also a teaching tool for meeting later needs, and a way to advocate and disclose on their own, as adults.

Both of these books, as well as my autobiography, *Beyond the Wall: Personal Experiences with Autism and Asperger's Syndrome*, also have useful information on successfully choosing a college or university and staying there.

In 2008, I completed my doctoral dissertation focused on matching "best practices" to the needs of children on the autism spectrum. After spending a year traveling, consulting, and presenting, internationally, on issues related

199

to the autism spectrum, I was approached by Adelphi University on Long Island, New York, to apply for a faculty position, teaching courses in special education and autism.

My interview with them was successful. I was hired "while autistic," meaning they had done their research on my experiences and what I had to offer. Therefore, I didn't have to do any careful dancing about disclosing my position on the autism spectrum, nor have to convince them why hiring someone on the autism spectrum might be good for teaching courses on that subject. Rather, they made their decision on whether I was a good match for them.

We may be headed, starting in higher education, into a new era where people on the autism spectrum are appreciated for what they are able to contribute to society, rather then focusing on differences and weaknesses. The future is here. People with autism are being considered as part of the diversity of the human gene pool, and use their strengths to live a fulfilling and productive live.

About the Author: Stephen Shore has Asperger's, is a professor at Adelphi University, and earned the following degrees: Ed.D. in Education, Boston University (2008); M.A. in Music Education, Boston University (1992); B.A. in Music Education, University of Massachusetts at Amherst (1986); B.A. in Accounting and Information Systems, University of Massachusetts at Amherst (1986); Ed.D. (2008) Boston University. You can learn more about him and his speaking events at www.autismasperger.net.

Chapter 20

Careers

Chapter 20
Careers

Help Your Child Build an Enriching Career

Parents, you are the bridge between your child's needs and educating employers and the community about autism.

...encourage professionals to talk the same language...

—Dr. Kathleen Quill

Most people with autism are detail oriented and extremely focused. They make loyal and dedicated employees. Help your child choose a career according to strengths, interests, and aptitude. In many cases, it is a good idea to get a mentor and a career analysis for your child.

Parent Tip: Do not pressure your child to perform or succeed.

Remember, career decisions may be a team effort, but your child should have the final say.

Jobs such as engineering, library science, accounting, inventory control, and banking are excellent choices for those who lean towards math and science. High visual learners gravitate towards careers such as digital photography, video game development, and multi-faceted artistic endeavors.

Many on the spectrum have gone the vocational school route and do well in jobs like auto mechanics, hairdressing, carpentry, design, plumbing, and all aspects of computer technology.

Multi-tasking type jobs tend to be self-defeating for many people on the spectrum, because of their ability to focus so well. That said, check to see if there is a match between your child's abilities and interests in any job, especially waiting tables, stock trading, and fast-paced sales jobs. Check with your child very carefully before he or she enters a position requiring long-term memory skills, as some people on the spectrum find this challenging.

Happily, people with autism are making up a growing portion of the labor pool. Employers are enhancing work environments for those on the spectrum and appreciating their new employee's talents and gifts.

> **Parent Tip:** Career planning for your child must begin well before high school. Find out which courses match your child's interests and career choice.

Here Are Some Good Things to Think About Before Job Seeking

- Know your child's desires, skills and interests

- Have your child sign up for courses that will help make the transition to work easier

- Learn about transportation and living arrangements

- Involve the community and talk with friends about references

- Make sure that your child's IEP team has career and employment development experts as team members

- Help your child find a job mentor

Seeking employment may prove to be a difficult task because your child is putting himself or herself entirely on the line, exposing some limitations and risking possible rejection.

You may want to use social stories, scripting and role-playing with your child before they go on a job interview. Review all the points that employers notice and consider before hiring any employee.

Ensure your child fully understands each of the following items before job hunting or interviewing

- On-time behavior

- Personal hygiene

- Appropriate dress

- How to present concrete goals and list strengths

- How to anticipate and respond to an employer's questions

- How, specifically, to disclose autism or autism traits

- What to say and how to discuss special needs, such as lighting, quiet places, times for breaks, sensory issues, social skills and more...

- How to approach fellow coworkers socially and for work-related items

- Ways to present "skills" as the reason to hire

- Maintain a portfolio of accomplishments

- Create the proper resume to match the job and your child's interests

Hooray, your child landed the job! Now what?

Be the bridge between your child and the employer. Here is a checklist of talking points you can review with your child and your child's employer before the first day of work:

- Many with autism are hypersensitive to noise, fluorescent lights, scents or even strong textures. They operate better in an enclosed office space, not open floor plans.

- We recommend replacing the lights in your home, office or dorm room with full spectrum lights. Full spectrum means you can see all colors, just as if you were outdoors. Regular lights are more yellowish and the human visual system gets overloaded with stimuli with a high blinking or refresh rate on the fluorescent lights. In addition, regular or fluorescent lights do not allow you to see all the colors as you should, and in darker climates, with gray skies, it's easier to suffer from Seasonal Affective Disorder (SAD), with the wrong lighting.

- According to Dr. Julian Whitaker (Health & Healing, Vol.2,No.13,12/92), "Light enters your eyes and has a stimulatory effect on your hypothalamus, pineal gland, and pituitary gland-the master hormone-secreting gland of the body. Lights that approximate the sun's full spectrum of energy keep your glands stimulated, happy, and healthy. Lights that do not, can make you sick".

- Since conventional lighting has an unbalanced spectral distribution, distorting colors with a greenish-yellowish hue, it stresses our eyes, and creates an unpleasant atmosphere. This unbalanced light can produce imbalances in us.

- People with autism, and others, are especially sensitive to the blink rate in fluorescent lights. This constant, rapid blinking, according to the work of Dr. John Ott and others, suggests that it affects the brain, visual processing and gives people headaches. Others note that they feel fatigued, the more time they spend working under fluorescent lights.

- We recommend GE Reveal Lights, and lights from Gaiam, which recreate real daylight, where you see the full spectrum of colors. You can get the Reveal lights at most grocery stores or places like Home Depot. Gaiam, at www.gaiam.com carries a large array of natural daylight items, as well as ergonomically correct balance ball chairs, which puts people the correct alignment when sitting as a desk or table. These are very inexpensive ways for your child to feel more relaxed.

Tips For Employers and Managers

- Employers, managers and coworkers may need to change the way they speak with an employee who has autism. Your employee may not understand typical jokes, sarcasm, or colloquialisms.

- Your employee with autism may seem disinterested in other people, and you'll want to foster good relations between everyone in your company, so you may need to train others how to understand various personalities of those with autism.

- Many on the spectrum have trouble working on teams. They miss social cues like gestures, facial expressions, and tone of voice. One particular employee might get interested in one thing and talk about it incessantly.

- Routine is important. Changes are very disruptive and upsetting.

- Body language does not always mean the same to autistics as it does to neuro-typicals. Employers and coworkers should not take lack of eye contact or unusual facial expressions personally.

- The employer should always be direct and very specific with instructions and expectations. Use lists, schedules and even pictures, as much as possible.

- The person with autism may need extra time to finish a task and/or may become overloaded with too much work or responsibility. Check in, on a regular basis, to determine if this happens and make adjustments.

- Employers and coworkers need to be sensitive to how they speak in front of the person with autism. Using labels like "the autistic guy" is not appropriate. Neither is talking in front of the autistic person as if he or she were not present.

With minor effort on the part of management, a person with autism can be a highly valuable asset to your business. Employees with autism may bring high intelligence, high-level writing skills, immense interest in various components of your company and a high degree of visual, big picture overviews which may ultimately lead to increased productivity.

If you become more aware, and help others in your company to become more understanding, everyone in your organization will experience a higher quality work environment, and one which enables the desire to continue working at your company.

Chapter 21

Aging

Chapter 21

Aging

Bill Davis

There are many issues associated with aging parents who have children with autism. For example, as parents age, therapies and medical attention become even more significant for their adult children with autism. My wife, Kate, and I have a vision for residential facilities where aging parents can live with their autistic children.

...he will always know that he is loved and that he will always be safe

—Nancy H Cale

Counseling, fitness, activities, and recreation in these facilities will result in a strong staff-child bonding. Thus, if you live in a residential facility with your child, it ensures a smooth transition for your child when you pass away.

Age tends to bring poor health and uncertainty for the future, raising new questions like who we can trust to care for our children. Others questions relate to where finances come from, where your child will live, plus all the items listed in Chapter 14 on financial planning.

My son, Chris, will outlive me. I am plagued with uncertainly, even though I've done everything I know of to assure myself that he will be well cared for and safe. Yet, I still stay awake at night sometimes wondering who will tuck Chris in, scrub his handsome face, and comb his hair just right. Who will preserve his purity and protect his innocence? My God, who will hold him, soar when he smiles and write his schedule? Who will love him?

As parents, we work with, and care for our children until we basically break down. At that point, if you're not prepared, you are faced with very limited options, so best to plan far ahead on this one.

Parent Tip: Start planning your family's future now. Demand programs, seek legal advice and community resources to help your child prepare for independence.

Early intervention, setting up living arrangements, employment, training, and community services help alleviate our fears. Begin researching now. Don't procrastinate. Arrange for both you and your child. Get exercise, recreational activities, and a hobby. In addition, secure respite care.

You can uphold your child's interests in community activities via your pre-planning process. Carry your child's ID card, as well as all contact and behavioral information with you at all times, so your child is protected should something happen to you. Inform neighbors and as many people in the community as you can, so your child, young or older, is safe. Enroll your child in self-advocacy training. Do not neglect training your first responders. Set up housing, job training, life skills and service committees. Collect information on state and local resources and meet with local advocates and mentors regularly.

Our children are as unique as the autism spectrum. They require flexible services. With the autism population growing so quickly, we face epidemic numbers of aging parents. An autism-friendly community will flourish and be enriched. A seamless system will bring all available options to parents and persons with autism. Parents should begin serving on boards that deal with autism. Get involved in your community and government, regarding every topic about autism, including aging.

Karen's Comments: Just as flowers, we sprout, blossom and bloom, but eventually fade to the dust we once were. It is important to set up a plan so we can empower our children to be as self-sufficient and self-moderating as possible, thus enriching the quality of their life.

Chapter 22

Epilogue

Chapter 22

Epilogue

Keri Bowers

When I was asked to write the epilogue for *Autism Tomorrow*, I wasn't sure how such a book as this could possibly end. Generally, an epilogue is placed at the end of a piece of literature or drama in order to bring closure to the work. But, let us be real. In autism, is there really such thing as closure? At least I do not think so.

Autism tomorrow lives in the choices we make today

—Keri Bowers

I like the word "epilogue" anyway, so I agreed to take pen in hand and attempt this effort. Still I kept coming back to one thing: there is no closure in autism, there is only moving forward each and every day. In turn, this begged of me – no, screamed at me – that I ask what I believe is the most important question of all:

"WHAT NOW?" Yep, that's it... "WHAT NOW?"

In reading *Autism Tomorrow*, you are gifted to read the words, thoughts, ideologies, experiences, and expertise of some of the greatest minds in autism today. People who are transforming possibilities in autism around the world, all here in one book, and right before your eyes! Poignant, powerful words and experiences that likely had you cry silently or out loud on one page, and laugh or chuckle on the next… "Yeah, my kid did that too!" We can relate, yes? And yet, no matter what your "politics" are in autism, I think we can all agree on one thing: that our common goal in autism is opportunity, inclusion, growth and development for our children. And so, here is the amazing thing about all of the information contained in this book: This information is a call to action!

So now, as you close the final pages of this book, you can consciously, and with effort, allow the new ideas and information you received to create a new framework to help you to design what autism looks like for you and your child tomorrow.

So how can the new information you've learned here help to move you and your child forward? What might autism look like in your world as your child grows? These are very important questions to ask of the mind and the spirit.

As a mother of a 21 year old with high functioning autism, I didn't always ask myself the question, "What now?" In fact, back in what I call the "dark ages of autism," my questions were more like: "Why me?" and "Why my boy?"

I was racked by pain, sorrow, and what I call my "death of a dream." I had not yet overcome the sadness, madness and confusion I felt over having a child who was different - even "defective" as I secretly felt at the time. It seemed in the beginning, life with my boy Taylor, was more like an end. And then one day I had an outrageous experience; even for a creative, if not airy-fairy, woman like me. It was much like an out of body experience, but this experience was real.

Words from my diary when Taylor was a year and a half old, circa 1990 - the voice said… "Why not you, Keri?"

As I lay alone in the dark, I cry out to God. "Why God... Why me?" These are desperate cries from a desperate mother. Tears wet my pillow, and my fists are clenched in rage. How can this be happening to me? To my son?

Suddenly, out of nowhere it seems, I hear a small yet big voice. It says: "Why not you, Keri? Why not you?"

"What the…(expletive here deleted...) Where'd that come from?" I am not accustomed to hearing voices, let alone voices that clearly do not support my pity-pot.

This small, yet big voice is a sobering one. And, I think to myself: "Yeah, Keri, why not you?"

It is on this day that I vow I will never again ask "Why," but instead will ask: "What now?"

Taylor is still not yet walking, and he is not talking either, yet I feel "pink fuzzies" for the very first time.   5/24/1990

Today, my son is 21 years old, and does walk and talk, I am so thankful to say. By now, Taylor has made 3 films with me, and travels all over the world to share his story in life with autism. Incredibly (or not,) Taylor has achieved much more than I might have imagined if I had not reframed my self-talk all those years ago.

In looking back, I am clear that in reframing the central questions, it gave me the ability (and courage) to consciously chart (or "map"), a very different outcome than I would otherwise have experienced. Today, it is with a lot of hard work and thanks I say: "Thank you God, for that."

No matter where you are in your journey - whether you experience acceptance or anger; fear or hope; sorrow or joy, now that you have new information, here is the great news. You now have an amazing opportunity at your door to re-frame the core questions you ask of yourself. And, "What Now?" is a great place to start.

Whether you walk for the cure; advocate for vaccination reform; choose biomedical paths, work in conventional therapies or unconventional ones, or, like me, dance and paint in the world of the autistic mind, there is one common thread for each of us. Everyday we get up and face the baffling world of autism and figure out (consciously or unconsciously) our next move. Hopefully, this book has provided you with great ideas to do just that. So in this "epilogue," and as a partner in autism, I ask you to ask yourself. "What now?" and offer these practical parting tips to help you do this:

Assess what you do and do not believe in autism as it affects your child; your life. Be honest with yourself; there is no good, bad, right or wrong answer. Write a "mission statement" for your child and your family. Incorporate that mission everyday into your emotional and physical world. Write down fears, hopes and dreams for your child. Get to know how you really feel inside; the good and the bad. Take action steps in an IEP, (Individualized Education Program), IPP (Individual Program Plan), ISP (Individualized Service Plan), MTPs (Master Treatment Plan) and any other "p" that comes your way to "live in" to your mission statement. Attend all meetings from a place of collaboration rather than defense. Bring croissants or donuts (it lightens up the mood.). Find support in others – every good athlete needs a coach. Keep an open mind. We don't need to make others wrong, in order for us to be right.

Write down where you see your child in 5, 10, 15 years. Ask others about their ideas for your child's future. Be open to their answers. They may see possibility or lack. Your goal is simply to ask open-ended questions to get a sense of what others see as possibilities. You will learn amazing things when you ask these questions! Continue to educate yourself; keep up on the latest in autism strategies and advancements. Be kind to those who do not totally agree with you - we are in this together. Know that every day is a new day even when the one before it might have been really crummy. Be gentle with yourself, your child, and others in your world. And finally…

…Breathe.

I do not think it is so much what we hope for, or pray for, think about, or want. In the reality of autism, it is about what we do today that will affect tomorrow. In mapping (or dreaming up) qualities for your child's future, I believe you can create possibilities beyond your wildest imagination. On a blank canvas, where nothing appears, I submit that all things are possible.

About the Author. Keri Bowers, is the creator of the hit films, Normal People Scare Me; the Sandwich Kid; & ARTS. Talks and workshops based on her workbook, "Mapping Transitions to Your Child's Future" have Keri traveling around the world to share her work in "possibilities, disabilities, and the arts." Her current film in production is called "Desire," a film about sexuality and disabilities. For more information about Keri's work, visit www.normalfilms.com

Autism Tomorrow Glossary

AAC — Augmentative and Alternative Communication, uses pictures or other means instead of words to help children communicate.

ABA — Applied Behavioral Analysis, a specific therapy and assessment for autism. ABA takes what we know about behavior and uses it to bring about changes of the behavior.

Axiom —A widely accepted or established proposition or statement.

ASA — Autism Society of America; raises and allocates funds, addressing many unanswered questions about autism.

ASD — Autism Spectrum Disorder, referring to the five types of autism; Asperger's Syndrome, Kanner's Syndrome, Pervasive Developmental Disorder - Not Otherwise Specified (PDD-NOS), Rett Syndrome, Childhood Disintegrative Disorder.

AHEADD — Achieving in Higher Education with Autism/Developmental Disabilities (aheadd.org). A private, community organization providing support for students with autism and developmental disabilities with higher education and independence.

Asperger's syndrome — An ASD, often accompanied by significant social skills, deficits, and repetitive patterns of behavior and interests.

Apraxia — Inability to perform complex movements, often as a result of brain damage, for example, following a stroke. Also called dyspraxia.

Autism Today— (autismtoday.org). Organization created in 1998 to provide information and resources for parents, educators, professionals, and those on the autism spectrum.

Autism Speaks — (autismspeaks.org) Science and advocacy organization dedicated to funding research for the causes, prevention, treatments, and a cure for autism.

B12 — A water-soluble vitamin that plays a key role in the normal functioning of the brain and nervous system. B12 is often deficient in children with autism, along with Vitamin-A, sulfate, calcium.

B12 a supplement to help intestinal (GI) issues, food allergies, and digestion problems.

Boardmaker — (mayer-johnson.com) Software program used to help adults and children with autism communicate. Boardmaker uses picture communication symbols to create printed communication boards..

Casein — Predominant phosphoprotein in all bovine dairy products, often not digestible in those with autism, resulting in opiate-like affect in the brain.

Celiac disease — Disease of the small intestine damaged from grains containing gluten, such as wheat, barley, rye, and some oats.

Colored Overlays — Tranparency overlays, which, when placed over print, may clear up visual distortion, and help readers be more fluent, and have an easier time reading. Overlays are found at: www.HowToLearn.com/filters.html

Cortisol — Corticosteroid hormone or glucocorticoid produced by the adrenal cortex, which is part of the adrenal gland. It is usually referred to as the "stress hormone" as it is involved in response to **stress** and **anxiety**.

Chelation therapy — Type of therapy used to remove heavy metals from the body. EDTA is injected into the blood, which binds metals and allows them to be removed from the body through the urine.

Coprolalia — Uncontrollable use of obscene language; often accompanied by mental disorders, typical in those with Tourette's syndrome.

Developmental Optometrist (also known as Behavioral or Neuro-Optometrist — Developmental optometrists are optometrists who examine patients for the health of the eye, and are also certified, after additional years of training, to examine patients to determine how well their entire visual system functions. These eye doctors want to know whether patients have the additional skills neeeded to read, write, play sports, and do a whole host of other things related to their everyday life. You may find developmental optometrists at www.covd.org or www.oep.org

DPT vaccine — Immunization or vaccine to protect against the diseases diphtheria, pertussis, and tetanus. Five doses are commonly given to children between the ages of two months to five years old, providing lifelong immunity to diphtheria and pertussis, but DPT does not provide lifelong immunity to tetanus.

DMPs — (Sodium 2,3-dimercaptopropane-1-sulfonate); used since 1960 to treat heavy metal toxicity, such as zinc, copper, arsenic, mercury, cadmium, lead, silver, and tin. Mercury toxicity by intravenous injection.

DMSA — (meso-2, 3-dimercaptosucccinic acid); a mercury-chelating agent, which penetrates the brain cells.

DMG — Supplements that support mental alertness and brain function during periods of stress. May also reduce seizures.

Elijah's Cup — Valerie Paradiz' book *Elijah's Cup: A Family's Journey into the Community and Culture of High-Functioning Autism and Asperger's Syndrome*, containing insightful material about self-esteem.

ESY — Extended School Year. Eligibility is determined by the child's Individualized Education Program (IEP) team that determines whether a child needs extended school year services in order to receive Free Appropriate Public Education (FAPE).

Flapping — Repetitive motion used to show excitement and/or emotions where arms or hands flap. An activity often found in those with autism.

Fight-or-flight response — The human body's automatic response that prepares the person to "fight" or "flee" from what it perceives as an attack or threat. Emotional effects of fight-or-flight response are; anxiety, poor concentration, depression, frustration, anger, sadness, fear, and hopelessness. Others stress-induced conditions are eye twitching or teeth grinding. People with autism become super sensitive and notice every detail, however lack the ability to prioritize.

Fade — When a person with autism sort of *disappears* or *spaces out* emotionally while still physically present.

FAPE — Free Appropriate Public Education; an educational right of children in the United States with disabilities, as part of the IEP, guaranteed by the IDEA.

HFA — High Functioning Autism; informal term applied to those with higher functioning autism (Asperger's) than other autistic people.

Hyperlexia – Exceptional ability to recognize words with no understanding or comprehension of them, common in those with Asperger's.

Inter Vivos Trust —Revocable trust used to guard and plan a child's future. It can be funded with portions of estate, life insurance, IRAs, as well as cash.

IEP — **Individualized Education Program** (IPP in Canada) Detailed description of a special education student's educational goals, method of assessment, and behavioral management plan. Visit www.wrightslaw.com for more information.

Icons — Visual (pictures) form of communication your child can use with parents, school or in the community.

Institute on Disabilities, Temple University — **(temple.edu)** Located in Philadelphia, PA, one of the sixty-seven University Centers for Excellence in developmental disabilities education, research and service, funded by the Administration on Developmental Disabilities, U.S. Department of Health and Human Services. This institute is a national leader in disability studies, leadership development, assistive technology, justice for people with disabilities, augmentative communication, and emergency preparedness.

IDEA — Individuals with Disabilities Education Act. Autism was added in 1990. The Education for All Handicapped Children Act (P.L. 94-142) of 1975 and the Individuals with Disabilities Education Act (IDEA) (P. L. 101-476) identified specific categories of disabilities under which children may be eligible for special education and related services. As defined by IDEA, the term "child with a disability" means a child with: mental retardation, hearing impairments (including deafness), speech or language impairments, visual impairments (including blindness), serious emotional disturbance, orthopedic impairments, autism, traumatic brain injury, other health impairments, or specific learning disabilities; and whom, by reason thereof, needs special education, and related services.

Kinesthesia — Ability to perceive change in body position, movement and muscular tensions, etc.

Kennedy Krieger Institute: Center for Autism — (kennedykrieger.org) Baltimore-based, multi-faceted institute that is a multidisciplinary program for children with autism spectrum disorders and their family members.

Language Acquisition through Motor Planning (LAMP) — Therapeutic approach to teach non-verbal individuals to communicate based on neurological and motor skills learning principles.

Learning Styles — Learning styles are the various modalities through which a person prefers to process new information. The most common learning styles are visual (thinking in pictures), auditory (learning through listening) and kinesthetic (learning through tactile means). There is a free Personal Learning Styles Inventory at www.HowToLearn.com

LRE — Least Restrictive Environment; in compliance with IDEA, a learning environment where a disabled student has the opportunity to be educated with non-disabled students to the greatest extent possible.

Letter of Intent — Not a legal document (except in adjunct to a will), which provide courts or care providers with an insight into what daily life should be like for your child in your absence. This document outlines daily schedules, enjoyable activities, social preferences, religious beliefs, and future living arrangements. It may also include the hopes, dreams, and desires of your child.

M.I.N.D. Institute — Medical Investigation of Neurodevelopmental Disorders; an international, multidisciplinary research organization committed to excellence, collaboration, and hope, and strives to understand the causes and develop better treatments and ultimately cures for neurodevelopmental disorders.

NICHCY — (nichcy.org) National Information Center for Children and Youth with Disabilities; a resource for parents who believe their child's school is out of compliance as outlined in the IEP. An excellent resource for regulations, time constraints, and procedures.

Neurotypical sibling — a brother or sister who does not have autism.

Non-verbal learning disorder (NLD) — Delay in understanding or using the spoken word. Difficulty with simple instructions, naming simple things, motor coordination, and limited attention span. Older children display difficulty differentiating right and left, and reverse letters, numbers, or words. They also lack motor skills to do everyday tasks.

People on the spectrum — The autism spectrum (autism spectrum disorder-ASD); describes characteristics such as abnormalities of social interactions, difficulty with communication, repetitive behavior, etc.

Perseverate — Strong focus. Doing certain actions over and over again, i.e. repeating a phrase, opening and shutting a door, twiddling fingers, lining up toys, rubbing hands together, spinning objects, etc.

PECS — Picture Exchange Communication System; augmentative and alternative communication (AAC) that uses pictures instead of words to help children communicate, designed especially for children with autism who have delays in speech development.

Pica — Pattern of eating non-food materials, such as dirt or paper. Children and adults with pica may also eat animal feces, clay, dirt, hairballs, ice, paint, and sand.

Probiotics — Dietary supplement of beneficial bacteria (live microorganisms), thought to increase immunity and improve digestion.

Pressure — Applying compressive force to portions of the body, with either hands or objects, such as blankets, to provide therapy for a person with autism. Deep pressure may have a calming effect for persons with autism, especially those with high levels of arousal or anxiety.

Red flags — Red flags of autism; visit AutismSpeaks.org for a list of indications for which a child is at risk for atypical development, and possibly in need of immediate evaluation by a pediatrician or family practitioner.

Stim/stimming — Repetitive body movements that are self-stimulating to one or more of the senses.

Dr. Stephen Shore — Author of *Beyond the Wall: Personal Experiences with Autism and Asperger's Syndrome*. Dr. Shore is a professor of special education at Adelphi University, and a world renowned speaker, who has Asperger's and focuses on helping people with ASD.

Stereotypy — Repetitive, persistent and ritualistic movement, posture, or utterance, often found in those with autism spectrum disorders.

SNT — The Special Needs Trust (SNT) is a legal document that provides for the needs of a disabled person without disqualifying him or her from benefits received from programs such as Social Security, Medicaid, SSI, subsidized housing, and other government benefits.

Self-advocates — Principle and/or practice of allowing those with disabilities to assume practical and legal responsibility for their own lives.

SSI — Supplemental Security Insurance; a federal program designed to supplement the income of the disabled, to provide means for shelter, clothing and food.

Social stories — Method used by parents and teachers to describe the desired behavior and the reinforcement of consequences.

Self-injurious — State of hurting one's self, deliberate or otherwise.

Scripting — Written communication. Can be **a vi**able tool to help your child communicate more easily.

Self-model — Parent or teacher demonstrating how to do something so the child can replicate the action on his own.

Dr. Temple Grandin — a Doctor of Animal Science and professor at Colorado State University, bestselling author, and consultant to the livestock industry in animal behavior. As a person with high-functioning autism, Grandin is also widely noted for her work in autism advocacy and is the inventor of the hug machine designed to calm hypersensitive persons.

Typical person/sibling — Sister or brother who does not have autism

TEACCH — (teacch.com) Treatment and Education of Autistic and related Communication-handicapped Children; an evidence-based service, research program and training, for individuals with ASD.

Toe walking — Method of walking on ones toes, without applying weight on the heel or the rest of the foot.

Thank You To Our Friends and Partners!

We sincerely thank all our partners and friends
who helped spread the word about *Autism Tomorrow*

Autism Speaks — www.AutismSpeaks.org

Autism Today — www.AutismToday.com

Frank Barnhill, M.D. — www.ADHDbehavior.com

Keri Bowers — www.NormalFilms.com

The Center For AAC & Autism — www.AACandAutism.com

Eric Chessen — www.AutismFitness.com

C.O.V.D. – Locate Developmental Optometrists — www.Covd.org

Bill Davis — www.Facebook.com/bill.davis.pa

John Dowson — www.Life-Trust.com

Forest Hills Financial Group, Nathan Perlmutter — www.fhfg.com

Temple Grandin — www.TempleGrandin.com

Stephen Guffanti, M.D. — www.RocketPhonics.com

Sharon Hensel-Cohen — www.NickysWorld.com

Katya Hill — www.aacinstitute.org

Lea Hill — www.LeaMHill.com

KEEN Foundation.org — www.KeenFoundation.org

Rebecca Kochenderfer — www.Homeschool.com

Joel Manzer — www.Autisable.com

Julie Matthews — www.NourishingHope.com

O.E.P. — www.OEPF.org

Kumar Ramlall, M.D. — www.ThinkTAction.com

David Riklan — www.SelfGrowth.com

Prentke Romich — www.PrentRom.com

Kim Schnepper & Martin Cherrin — www.fhfg.com/fhfvideo2.cfm

Stephen Shore — www.AutismAsperger.net

Susan Simmons — www.SimmonsGallery.com

Pete and Pam Wright — www.Wrightslaw.com

Pat Wyman — www.HowToLearn.com

Autism Tomorrow Resources — www.AutismTomorrowResources.com

Autism Tomorrow Sponsorship — www.AutismTomorrowSponsors.com

Age of Autism – Daily web newspaper about autism — www.AgeOfAutism.com

AutismOne.org – Nonprofit blog to educate parents about autism — www.AutismOne.org

Autism Society of America – Raises, allocates funds for autism — www.Autism-Society.org

Autism Speaks – Nonprofit focusing on preventing autism — www.AutismSpeaks.org

Autism Today – Recommended Reading List — www.AutismToday.com/Booklist.html

Frank Barnhill, M.D. – ADHD and autism resources — www.ADHDbehavior.com

The Center For AAC & Autism – Center which improves language and communication skills
    — www.AACandAutism.com

Colored Overlays – Transparencies improve reading — www.HowToLearn.com/filters.html

C.O.V.D. – Locate Developmental Optometrists — www.Covd.org

DAN Doctors – List of biomedical physicians — www.Autism.com

Eric Chessen – Autism fitness products and services — www.AutismFitness.com

General Electric – Reveal® full spectrum lights — www.GE.com

Greens +, Sam Graci's alkalizing green drink and supplements — www.GreensPlus.com

Homeschool.com – Homeschooling Resources and Information for Everyone

KEEN Foundation empowers children with exceptional needs to reach their fullest potential
    — www.KeenFoundation.org, LHill@keenfoundation.org

LDOnline – Special needs resources — www.LDOnline.org

National Autism Association – Advocacy — www.NationalAutismAssociation.org

Normal Films – Films about special needs and more — www.Normalfilms.com

O.E.P. – Nonprofit resources and list of developmental optometrists — www.OEPF.org

PAVE – Parents Active For Vision Education — www.PaveVision.org

Nathan M. Perlmutter – Forest Hills Financial Group — www.fhfg.com

Prentke Romich – Communication devices and products — www.Prentrom.com

RaisingSmallSouls.com – Blog resource for parenting emotionally healthy children

Rocket Phonics – organization devoted to enhancing reading — www.RocketPhonics.com

SelfGrowth.com – Self growth topics with autism expert — www.SelfGrowth.com

SketchUp – Google's 3D model software — http://sketchup.google.com

Wrightslaw – Reliable special education resources and law — www.Wrightslaw.com

Give The World Your Heart
Proudly Supports *Autism Today*

Count your child's heart beats will they are doing positive activities such as the suggestions below

<u>Watch the counter grow!</u>

- **Drink Clean Water**
- **Eat Nutritious Foods**
- **Exercise to Your Ideal Health**
- **Pray with Positive Gratitude Heart Beats**
- **Earn Your Sustainable Future**
- **Serve Your Community to Volunteer**
- **Trust in a Positive Healthy World**

Visit the World Gratitude Heart Beat Counter

at www.AutismToday.com/Heartbeat
Group login: autismtoday
Password: iampositive

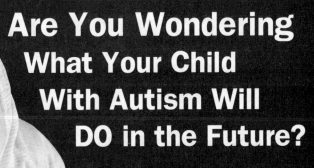